Sahaja Yoga-
The Secret to Self-Unfoldment and Transformation

Saraswati Raman

AuthorHouse™ UK Ltd.
500 Avebury Boulevard
Central Milton Keynes, MK9 2BE
www.authorhouse.co.uk
Phone: 08001974150

© 2011 Saraswati Raman. All rights reserved.

No part of this book may be reproduced, stored in
a retrieval system, or transmitted by any means
without the written permission of the author.

First published by AuthorHouse 1/26/2011

ISBN: 978-1-4567-7147-8 (sc)

Any people depicted in stock imagery provided by Thinkstock are models,
and such images are being used for illustrative purposes only.
Certain stock imagery © Thinkstock.

This book is printed on acid-free paper.

Because of the dynamic nature of the Internet, any Web addresses or
links contained in this book may have changed since publication and
may no longer be valid. The views expressed in this work are solely those
of the author and do not necessarily reflect the views of the publisher,
and the publisher hereby disclaims any responsibility for them.

Contents

Introduction	1
What is Sahaja Yoga?	9
About the Founder-Shri Mataji Nirmala Devi	11
The Subtle Systems of the Human body	15
How to develop vibratory awareness in Sahaja Yoga ?	20
Divine Discrimination	29
Likes and dislikes	34
Giving and Generosity	38
Forgiveness	41
Trust	44
Our Growth is our own responsibility	46
Guilt	48
Criticism	52
Creating positive patterns of thought and behavior	55
Intuition and vibratory awareness	60
Purity of Dedication to your Goal	64
Stress Management through Sahaja Yoga	74
Sahaja Yoga and Management	80
Sahaja Yoga and Music	87

Sahaja Yoga and Treatment of Diseases	96
Recognitions from the world	108
A Vision for the Future	110

Introduction

Our beloved Mother Shri Mataji Nirmala Devi, who gave us the secret knowledge of Kundalini, taught us how to experience the cool breeze that establishes our connection with the all pervading Cosmic power and encouraged us to experiment with the Nirmal Vidya that has transformed the way we understand things confronting us. As she says, when the drop becomes the ocean, it is the ocean that is going to nourish us, strengthen us and guide us but this can happen only when the connection between the drop and the ocean is fully established by dissolving into the greatness of the ocean, so also it is only the sincere desire of a sahaja yogi to be collective that can bring about this expansion of his being.

Coming from a drop status, we still continue to be engulfed by the past memories of the limitations of a drop. But the sharpness of attention developed through thoughtless awareness and doubtless awareness will enable us to closely observe our patterned responses and behavior and with patience we can attempt to change the counter productive patterns and cultivate more pleasant and finer qualities.

Becoming increasingly sensitive to others and

understanding them, by not being judgmental, being tolerant and responding based on an insight about our own shortcomings will lighten the load of suppressed emotion that we have been carrying with us over the years. A letting go of the emotional guard that once adorned our faces will allow us to express our finer qualities and true feelings in a more genuine way. With a greater awareness as to what is working against our higher nature, we can work at neutralizing them and focus on enhancing and nurturing the human element in our relationships and life in all its aspects.

This understanding of what Sahaja yoga has brought about in us can be carried forward to its next level so as to make it a part of our everyday life; can happen only if we are sincere in our efforts.

What does it mean to have large heartedness? Shri Mataji says that the heart has seven auras just like the brain which actually control the thinking pattern of the brain. The brain has two institutions- that of conditioning and ego. When a person becomes too egoistic, the auras of the brain get pressed and the heart is unable to influence the thinking process. With diminished usage, the auras of the heart become smaller and smaller, and ultimately disappear to make a person stone hearted. The heart is sensitive while the brain is not. When the heart is boiled in the heat of brain waves, it starts hating people, making us say harsh, hurting and sarcastic words to them. Conditionings of the brain make a person sly and perverted. Conditioning and ego boosts the brain and freezes the heart thereby making us forget how to be reassuring, protecting and nourishing to others.

With self-realization and Kundalini awakening, the kundalini moves upwards to touch the Brahmarandra which is the seat of the heart. And when that happens all the hurt that we have endured and suffered over ages, get dissolved and disappears. After this the heart starts functioning. We should then work on enlarging the heart's auras to engulf as many sahaja yogis as possible. This will ultimately bring about large heartedness where we can place our Mother, surrender to Her and worship Her.

Acknowledgements

In Sahaja yoga we have a way of saying that Shri Mataji gets it done through us, and that very process itself is the teaching process, and I, with all my heart and soul bow down to that learning, that teaching, that process what has now come to be known as Nirmal Vidya. Every experience is a learning, and my first and foremost acknowledgement of gratitude goes to that life process itself that has taught me the nuances that has culminated in the writing of this book. Many have been my teachers in this journey of life but the one that I hold dearest, who has been like a crystal clear, impartial and unbiased mirror, one who reflected back to me all that I was, all that I had gone through, all that I had suppressed, endured and fought with, one who stood by me as the enfoldment took place, is A D Nikam, to whom I shall be eternally thankful.

I would like to also place on record the immense courage and faith that was instilled in me from childhood by my mother, Smt. Vijayalakshmi Raman, who had more faith in me than I had in myself at that time, which has now helped me in standing rock solid even amidst all adversities. How can I not thank my father, Mr. C. N. Raman, who taught me every time I faltered, when times were very trying, and everything seemed all uphill, who stood be me and said that it is in such times when you feel all low and lost, that you should never quit. These die hard kind of philosophies helped me pull through a near death like existence, who only I, apart from them, knew what it was all like.

I feel very thankful to my very scientifically-precise-thinking and living her life on her own terms kind of sister, Mrs. Savitri Murthy Bala, in distant lands and my very cool, enigmatic, and understanding kind of brother, Mr. R. Narayanan, both of whom I know will always be there for me when I need them.

I thank the many fellow travelers who have all in no small measure contributed to the learning of the living process that is Sahaja Yoga. I would like to particularly mention the names of Mr. Parag Raje and Mr. Arun Apte who made my experiences and growth in Sahaja yoga more meaningful and realistic.

I also fondly remember Mrs. Chandrika Nair, the very dedicated Principal of a school in Ambernath, who was very often my sounding board for ideas and plans and who responded very enthusiastically with all her leadership qualities that amply exuberated in her actions through her dedicated team of sahajis.

I am indeed grateful to Rasha, the author of the book "The Divine Wisdom of Oneness" who was so gracious to let me use some of the pictures with oneness messages, that appear in the book, thereby enhancing the meaning of the flow of thought expressed."

I cannot forget all my colleagues in Canara Bank,

where I have been working for the past 29 years and which has been my karma bhoomi for all my learning process.

This book is dedicated to that Adi Shakti residing in the hearts of all Seekers of Truth, liberation and ultimate fulfillment in life.

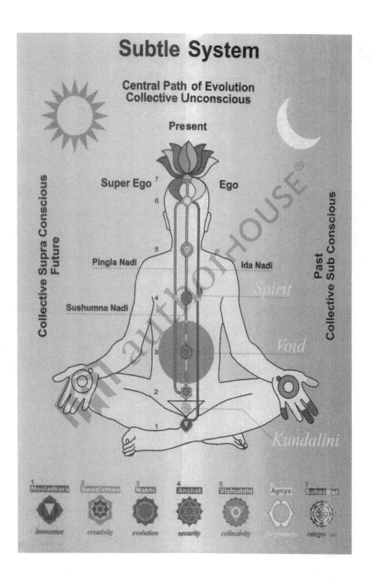

Chapter 1

What is Sahaja Yoga?

Sahaja yoga is a process of meditation wherein the sacred feminine energy called the Kundalini seated in the triangular sacrum bone becomes awakened and ascends through the seven subtle energy centers called as chakras, existing within every human being, and the individual Spirit becomes one with the universal Spirit. This is a process of Self Realization through the central channel or the Sushumna Nadi where the kundalini after being awakened pierces the seven chakras and emerges at the top of the head in the fontanel bone area and is felt as a gentle cool breeze.

Sahaja Yoga method of meditation brings a breakthrough in the evolution of human awareness. The mysterious kundalini energy accomplishes this herself and facilitates the blossoming of hitherto hidden, lost or forgotten qualities within us of pure innocence, spontaneity, creativity, security, compassion, collectivity, forgiveness and integration. Thus the transformation takes place within us. By this process a person becomes moral, united, integrated and balanced. As Shri Mataji says, "Sahaja yoga is different from other yoga because it begins with Self Realization ".

Through the practice of Sahaja Yoga, our awareness gains a new dimension where absolute truth can be felt tangibly – on our central nervous system. As a result of this happening, our spiritual ascent takes place effortlessly and physical, mental and emotional balance are achieved as a by product of this growth of our awareness. We then realize that we are not this body, mind, ego, conditionings, emotions or intellect, but something of an eternal nature which is always residing in our heart in a pure, undisturbed state as the Self or the Spirit. The Spirit is the source of true knowledge, peace and joy. Self Realization is the actualization of this connection with our Spirit, which as Shri Mataji advocates, is the birthright of every human being.

When the Kundalini power passes through each chakra, or psychic centre, the person will have complete control over the corresponding sense organs controlled by these chakras. Thus through her awakening an individual will become a completely balanced person, physically, mentally, emotionally and spiritually. So this feminine energy which is actually one's true mother makes a person absolutely integrated and fit to achieve his purpose in life

Chapter 2

About the Founder-Shri Mataji Nirmala Devi

Self Realization has always been the ultimate goal of all religions and spiritual traditions of the world, but was extremely difficult to attain in the past. Self Realization is the highest state achievable where individual consciousness is connected and united with universal consciousness. It has now become a mass phenomenon achieved effortlessly through the process known as Sahaja Yoga which is Shri Mataji Nirmal Devi's invaluable gift to humanity- a gift given at a time when hundreds of thousands of seekers all over the world are seeking the truth and hence are ready and equipped to receive this priceless gift from Adi Shakti Herself.

Shri Mataji Nirmala Devi was born on March 21 1923 to a Christian family in Chindwara, in Madhya Pradesh, India. Her parents were Prasad and Cornelia Salve, direct descendants of the royal Shalivahana dynasty. Seeing the beauty of this child who was born with a spotless brilliance they called her Nirmala, which means "Immaculate". Later on she came to be known by the multitudes by the name of Shri Mataji Nirmala Devi – the revered Mother who was born with her complete Self Realization and knew from a very young age that she had a unique gift which had to be made available to all mankind.

Her parents played a key role in India's Liberation Movement from under the British rule. Her father, a close associate of Mahatma Gandhi, was a member of the Constituent Assembly of India and helped write free India's first constitution. He was a renowned scholar, a master of 14 languages and translated the Koran in Marathi. Her mother was the first woman in India to receive the Honors Degree in Mathematics.

As a child, Shri Mataji lived with her parents in the ashram of Mahatma Gandhi. Gandhi saw the wisdom of this child and used to appreciate her immensely, affectionately calling her Nepali due to the Nepali features of her face. Shri Mataji's involvement in the freedom struggle is extremely remarkable. She was courageous and played a daring role as a youth leader of this campaign. She was even arrested and put into jail along with others during the 1942 Quit India Movement.

Shri Mataji was born with a complete understanding of the human nervous system and its energetic counterparts. In order to become acquainted with the scientific terminology associated with these subjects, she studied medicine and psychology at the Christian Medical College in Lahore.

Shortly before India achieved independence she married Sir. C. P. Srivastava, one of India's most dedicated civil servants, who were knighted by the Queen of England, and who served as Joint Secretary to the Prime Minister's office of the late Shri Lal Bahadur Shastri. Later he was elected for 16 consecutive years as the Secretary General of the United Nations International Maritime Organization.

As Sri C. P. Srivastava moved in fame from the Indian history to the worldly scene, Shri Mataji, after fulfilling her familial duty of bringing up her two daughters, embarked on her spiritual mission

On the 5th of May 1970, on a lonely beach of Nargol about 150 Kms from Mumbai) a divine spiritual experience filled her whole being and suddenly she found an answer to her question. She discovered a historical process of en-masse Self Realization through which thousands of people could get this connection to their Spirit and thereby achieve their inner transformation.

Shri Mataji made this experiment of awakening the spiritual power of every human being, which the Hindus call Kundalini, the Muslims as the Ruh and which the Bible describes as the Holy Ghost. She tried it first on the people near to her and noticed they were transformed physically, mentally and spiritually. Slowly she found out that only this process had the potential solution for all human problems and therefore decided to spread it on an en-masse level.

She invested her own time and money to talk to people and give them the key to their own spiritual power. Those few who started feeling this spiritual power , which flowed like a cool breeze over their whole body, especially over the palms of their hands and on top of their head around the fontanel bone area were quite astonished that it worked. Under the instructions of Shri Mataji they tried giving this power to others, which really gave them the faith that this was the true spiritual experience that was being prophesized in every religion.

Since 1970, Shri Mataji Nirmala Devi has traveled all around the world teaching the techniques of Sahaja Yoga ,absolutely free of cost, maintaining and insisting that one cannot pay for your enlightenment. Shri Mataji has dedicated her life to triggering the spiritual ascent of mankind through Self Realization, reclaiming the role of women in the spiritual evolution and guiding humanity to correct today's moral dilemmas.

Large number of people , without distinction of race, religion, age or social status has acknowledged the value of her teachings by establishing Sahaja Yoga centers in over 85 countries. These people who live a normal family life, tap into their inner spiritual power through daily Sahaja Yoga meditation and have achieved a complete balance in their lives on the physical, emotional, mental and spiritual level, through their direct and tangible experience on the central nervous system.

Chapter 3

The Subtle Systems of the Human body

The Three Channels

Anatomists describe two nervous systems in the human body – the cerebro- spinal and the sympathetic system. The cerebro--spinal begins with the brain, continues down the spinal cord, and ramifies to all parts of the body through the ganglia from which nerves issue between every two successive vertebrae. The sympathetic system consists of two cords which run almost the whole length of the spine, situated a little forward of its axis and to the right and left respectively. From the ganglia of these two cords, sympathetic cords proceed to form the network systems called the plexuses from which in turn, as from relay stations, emerge smaller terminal ganglia and nerves. In addition we have a third group called the vagus nerves, which arise in the medulla oblongata and descend independently far into the body, mingling constantly with the nerves and plexuses of the other systems.

Human beings cannot avoid these two influences. Each person carries two channels of energy, which reproduce the two great biological rhythms on the individual level. These are the Rajo guna or Yang, and the Tamo guna or Yin, which, together, correspond, in medical terms, to the sympathetic nervous system.

The Left Channel

Tamo guna, which is also known as the Ida nadi, or simply the "left channel", begins below the sacrum bone and ends in the right hemisphere of the brain. This corresponds to the left sympathetic nervous system, which Shri Mataji calls the "superego". It constitutes the feminine, lunar side of the personality. The Anima, as defined by Jung, is its reflection at the psychological level. This left channel controls our desire and emotions, and integrates all our previous experiences. It is responsible for remembering all the information acquired by education, information which is stored in the various strata of consciousness. This channel ensures, for instance, that a child who has suffered burning will not go too close to the flame of a candle again. It acts as a sort of "brake" on the personality.

It is this channel which prevents action that does not comply with the canons of morality, or with the conditioning acquired during life, particularly childhood. When an individual bends too much towards this side of the personality, inhibitions to action will outweigh the capacity to act. He or she will become lethargic, introverted, listless and even fearful. The main effect of alcohol and narcotic drugs is to swing the psyche towards this side of our nature. If a correction is not applied, the imbalance intensifies and can culminate in psychiatric disorders such as depression or schizophrenia. Self-destructive tendencies can increase and somatic diseases such as angina pectoris or cancer develop.

On the other hand, if this channel functions in a normal

and balanced way, the individual avoids depressive states and is joyful in all circumstances. This is usually true of children who have had the benefit of a normal, innocent and happy childhood.

The Right Channel

Rajo guna or Pingala nadi controls the masculine side of the personality. It begins at the level of the Swadisthan chakra, situated in the region of the right kidney, and ends in the left cerebral hemisphere, which Shri Mataji calls the "ego". It corresponds to the right-side sympathetic nervous system, and, for simplicity, we will refer to it as the "right channel". This is the channel of action and creativity on both the actual and the intellectual levels. This is Jung's Animus. The right channel made it possible for humankind to free itself from the constraints of nature and climate. It allowed mankind to organize societies, and, by developing technical abilities, to found the first civilizations. It is this channel that allows Man to project himself into the future, and to invent.

Where the left channel is the brake on human nature, the right channel is its accelerator. The right channel is essential because it allows humankind to take individual responsibility. In a way it is the "steering wheel" of the personality which makes it possible to undertake a course towards a destination. However we can only use this steering wheel if the learning and experience acquired through the left channel continue to give the information we need, to avoid dangers, and about the changes of direction the weather conditions demand.

An overactive right channel leads to excessive development of the ego, causing domination and the misuse of power. Aggression, destruction, wars and conquests all stem directly from the right channel activity. An unbalanced left side leads to self-destruction, while imbalances on the right, with their ego consequences, lead to the destruction of others. The right and left channels are the dual poles of the personality which, when in balance, allow the individual to lead a life of harmony.

Sushumna, the Middle Path

The Kundalini rises along the central channel, known in Sanskrit as the Sushumna Nadi. "In Sushumna, the breath leads the pure man into a pure world," says the Prashna Upanishad1. The Yogatattwa Upanishad confirms that: "The Breath rises in the Sushumna up to the crown of the head."2 Through Self-Realization, the balance between the right and the left channels is restored and inner harmony re-established. This is the first purifying work of the Kundalini.

Sushumna is the Middle Way the Buddha spoke of. It is the way of balance between the right and the left channels, the way of evolution. Human beings are normally slaves to their mental activity. Thoughts arise from two sources: the right hemisphere of the brain, the superego (an extension of the left channel) which recalls past events, or the left hemisphere of the brain, the ego (the prolongation of the right channel) which projects into the future.

During realization, the Kundalini absorbs the ego and the superego. Thoughts fade away. There is no past, no future. All that remains is reality, that is, the present.

And in the present the Spirit, shining in the heart, penetrates into the consciousness of the individual. The Spirit alone IS. Kundalini and the Self are One.

Chapter 4

How to develop vibratory awareness in Sahaja Yoga ?

Sahaja Yoga is all about the use of vibratory awareness. Through this we begin to feel the effects of our behavior and that of the environment on our subtle instrument. Through vibratory awareness we can diagnose problems at a very early stage and then use various Sahaja techniques to bring the spiritual body back in to balance and clear any obstructions that may develop.

Another great benefit of Sahaja Yoga is that we can help each other in a very real and tangible way. By developing our vibratory awareness we can diagnose the condition of each other's chakras (energy centers) and then take steps to remove any blockages, and restore the system back to health and normality.

WORKING ON EACH OTHER

When we work on each other we can discern this new vibratory awareness much more quickly and we begin to clearly experience the flow of vibrations either in the hands or around the body. This is because the flow of vibrations increases substantially and this has the effect of helping the Kundalini to rise higher and with greater force; it also takes us deeper into meditation.

Some people find it difficult at first to experience thoughtlessness for longer than few moments. Working on each other makes us go spontaneously into it.

Another marvel of working on each other is that as we work on and clear each other's chakras, we also clear our own. For example if you start to work on someone and find there is a catch (i.e. an obstruction) on the nabhi chakra and you give it a bandhan and some vibrations, this will also start to clear and open your own nabhi centre. It can be a source of great joy to experience these different vibrations flowing through you as you work on different centers.

Furthermore if you find you have got a particular blockage on one of the centers, e.g. vishuddhi, it is easier to clear by asking someone with a good vishuddhi to work on you. This is because as they will have stronger vishuddhi vibrations flowing through them, it will be easier for them to clear this centre for you.

PROCEDURE
1.Go into meditation

2.Put a bandhan on yourself and raise Kundalini

3.Put a bandhan on person receiving vibrations and raise their Kundalini

4.Bring their mechanism into balance.

5.Diagnose which chakra(s) needs working on

6.Put bandhan on ailing chakra(s) and give it vibrations

7.When cool, finish by putting on bandhans and raising Kundalini

A STEP BY STEP GUIDE

For the purposes of clarity we refer to the two parties as one giving vibrations and the other as receiving vibrations.

1.Go into meditation

Before we start working on anyone it is important to go into meditation first ourselves. We can do this by putting our attention on the top of our head and try to find that silence within. Ideally we should be in thoughtless awareness all the time when we are working on others as this will maximize the flow of vibrations and keeps us clear.

2.Put a bandhan on yourself and raise Kundalini

Stand behind the person you will be working on, put a bandhan and raise your Kundalini. Putting on a bandhan will protect our instrument, bring us into balance, bring our attention inside and help us get into a meditative state.

3.Put a bandhan on the person receiving vibrations and raise his Kundalini

Putting a bandhan on them will protect their instrument, bring them into balance, bring their attention inside and help them get into a meditative state.

4.Bring their mechanism into balance.

Put your right hand above their head and see if you feel

anything. You may feel some coolness above i.e. over their head or maybe some heat if things are working out. If Kundalini is not coming through, you can raise their Kundalini again to increase the flow.

Then put both your hands towards the photograph of Shree Mataji and determine what you feel on your own instrument. Next put your attention on the person receiving vibrations and put your right hands towards them. See if you feel anything different. We do this so as to separate our own catches from those of the person whom we are working on. It may be difficult at first but with practice you will find that this new vibratory awareness will start developing rather quickly. It is often necessary to bring the instrument of the person receiving vibrations into balance first. When you put your hands towards some people you may experience a difference in flow of vibrations in each hand. You may find, for example, coolness on the right and warmth or heaviness on the left, if the person tends to use his left side channel (Ida Nadi) too much. To bring this into balance raise the right and bring down the left until you feel an even flow in both hands.

Conversely you may feel warmth or tingling on the right hand and little or nothing in the left. This is often the case with people who predominantly use their right side but prefer not to use their emotional side very much. To bring this into balance raise the left and bring down the right. Such people are often over active. Doing this will make them feel much more relaxed and peaceful.

5.Diagnose which chakra(s) needs working on

When you have brought their instrument into balance again put your attention on the person to see what you feel. This time focus on the fingers and see if you can find out which chakra needs to be worked on; it may take several seconds to get a clear indication.

During the early stages when we are developing this skill we may feel very uncertain about exactly what we feel and it is very tempting to just ask another Sahaja Yogi who may have greater sensitivity; this does have some merits. To develop our own sensitivity it is important that we start to operate on what we actually experience ourselves. In the beginning when our sensitivity is developing we may find it difficult to separate our own catches from those of the person receiving vibrations, but with a little practice it does become easier Another way of diagnosis is to run your right hand over the chakras of the person receiving vibrations to see if you feel any areas giving off heat. Feeling these changes in temperature is often one of the first experiences of vibratory awareness for many people.

Some people find that at first they do not feel much on their hands but more on the body. This is especially the case if your left vishuddhi is not very clear as this interferes with the sensitivity of the hands. You may find that you feel other people's catches on your own body when you put your attention on them. Or alternatively some people can feel where the Kundalini is stopping and thereby ascertain where the catches are directly by using the attention. Use whichever works for you best to begin with, after a while you will be able to use all of these methods.

6.Put bandhan on ailing chakra(s) and give it vibrations

When you have worked out which chakra needs to be worked on then put a bandhan on it. This is always a clockwise motion from the front and anti clockwise from behind as this is the way in which the chakra is actually spinning on the horizontal plane.

Then give it some vibrations. This you do by taking vibrations from the photograph of Shree Mataji or even from the cosmic energy with the left hand and giving them to the chakra with the right hand. After a while the experience of vibrations flowing into the left and out of the right will be quite clear.

In between clearing each chakra, it is helpful to raise Kundalini again a few times to push any blockages that may have been loosened up and can be brought out through sahasrara chakra.

In addition to this you can use other methods such as candle treatment, mantras and draining the left or right side.

We can put a bandhan on a chakra with the candle or just hold the candle flame near the problem area and it will burn off any obstructions. After a while you can actually feel it sucking the bhada (catch) and clearing the obstruction. It is also very useful for clearing the whole left side, which you can do by moving the candle flame up and down the Ida Nadi (left side).

The left channel can be cleared and drained off of all impurities, heat or excess negativity by placing the right hand on the earth until you feel the clear vibrations on the left palm placed on the lap. Similarly the right channel can be cleared by lifting the left hand up towards the sky to drain the right side. In addition to draining the left and right channels, this action also clears the chakras that are obstructed on either the left or right side.

7.Finish by putting on bandhans and raising Kundalini

When the person you are working on has their Kundalini established in Sahasrara and their vibrations are flowing then you can bring the session to a close by raising their Kundalini three times and putting a bandhan on them.

When you have done this raise your own Kundalini and put a bandhan on yourself. It is usually a good idea to sit and meditate quietly for a few minutes after working on someone to settle yourself down and ensure that you stay in the centre.

WHAT TO DO IF YOU ARE NOT SENSING THE VIBRATIONS ?

Some of us take a little longer than others before we start feeling things very clearly on our hands. To develop our sensitivity it is very helpful to foot soak daily. However until we do clearly feel the vibrations we can adopt another more systematic approach.

Follow steps 1, 2, and 3 above and then systematically put bandhans on and give vibrations to all the chakras starting with mooladhara. This in itself will start to clear both the person receiving vibrations and yourself and will also make you more sensitive. Both of you will also start feeling the qualities of the chakras as you work on them in turn, and they start to open.

For example you will both experience:

After trying the above a few times and also being attentive to what you feel on your fingers, you will soon start feeling the vibrations on your hands .

ISSUES TO BEAR IN MIND

When we work on people we also have to exercise sensitivity of another kind. For example when we work on someone they are in meditation so we should try not to disturb them unnecessarily by trying to have a conversation with them, telling what to do, or asking sensitive questions. We can always have a friendly chat afterwards. Similarly when we find catches on the person receiving vibrations it is better to just try and clear them as during this process we act as channels for the Divine energy to flow.

There is often a temptation to start healing those we know who may be very ill. We should Endeavour to make our own instrument strong, as during the early stages of our Self Realization, our own instrument is often a little vulnerable and we have yet to learn how to keep ourselves clear. If there is someone you want to help it would be better to bring them to a meeting where they can get their Self Realization and then let them work it out using Sahaja Yoga methods.

Self Realization works out best in a collective situation where we all help each other. Sahaja Yoga is more than just a body of knowledge. Through vibratory awareness we start to experience life in a new way and by regularly getting involved in a workshop each week we can hasten the development of this new awareness and deepen our connection with the Spirit.

Besides Sahaja Yoga itself is such a relaxing, pleasant and enjoyable experience for both the person giving vibrations and the person receiving it, so let us experiment and enjoy.

(Endnotes)

1

Chapter 5

Divine Discrimination

2Our worth is determined not according to the power we possess but according to how we use that power. Within all of us lie several self-serving aspects of nature that was a part of the evolutionary process that each of us have undergone and some of these qualities may be either active or may be lying dormant waiting for the right conditions for self-expression. If these tendencies are of the lower aspects of nature it will only create conflicts and spread it to others, just like the ripples created by pebbles thrown into a pond have the effect of reaching the other side of the shore.

On the other hand, love which manifests in the form of care, concern, helping those in need, not out of any sense of duty, hope or reward but of a heartfelt desire to do so, has the power of connecting and allowing life to flow in joy.

Changing a pattern of behavior will call our intense working of the witness attitude. Witness attitude or sakshi bhava which can be developed through regular practice of Sahaja meditation, will enable us to observe our own responses to situations which are triggered off on account of age old patterns of neuro-muscular responses that have created particular pathways over long years of time some of which may even span several lifetimes. These pathways will continue to prompt the same pattern of behavior. Watching our response as and when the situations arise, and repeatedly correcting our reactions to negative stimulus will weaken the pathways and ultimately a time will come when due to the reconfiguration of the response patterns we will be once and for all free from the crippling patterns of negative behavior.

One might ask how can one modify the habitual dislike of a person who arouses nothing but irritation and start liking him. Mother says, put a sankocha like that of Shri Rama. While talking to each other educate yourself, train yourself to say things that are sweet and nice which will make the other person feel that this person is properly brought up in the Sahaja yoga tradition.

Instead of criticizing or passing judgments about the other person look for something admirable in him or her. This will modify the switching arrangement in your neural pathway. This, if done in a witness state and done repeatedly, will bring awareness in your observation which will change the pattern of behavior.

Divine discrimination is the blessing of a clean and pure Agnya chakra developed out of a sense of forgiveness of behaviors both of others and ourselves arising out of human weaknesses and conditionings. Conditionings that are accumulated through our experiences not only of this life time but over several life times, which are all are recorded in our subtle system, and communicated to the Kundalini energy color our responses when manifested at the Agnya chakra. That is why we respond in different ways to the same situation or differently

30

at various times. The root chakra, the energy center at the base of the spine or the Mooladhar sends messages based on these recordings to the subconscious that gets reflected in our responses. The Mooladhar chakra which is placed in the pelvic plexus is connected to the left and the right sympathetic nervous system. Keeping this chakra pure and chaste through right behavior and conduct, we can develop the right viveka or discrimination.

While meditating the Kundalini rises through the Sushumna Nadi in a Realized person provided both the right and the left sympathetic nervous system or the Ida nadi and the Pingala nadi are in balance. This can be checked by feeling if the flow of breath through both the nostrils is even or not, which is normal during sunrise and sunset. At other times, when the left nostril is blocked and you are breathing through the right nostril, while meditating, the Shakti rises through the right channel, the Sun channel, and the seeker might experience heat or burning around the neck. Again, as Shree Mataji says, if any effort is put in by obstinate abstinence or by indulgence, the excitement of the sympathetic activity starts, putting a pressure on the subject's attention causing it to move on the Ida or the Pingala Nadi. This causes terrible heat in the body and one may suffer from restlessness. Instead of rising to the thoughtless awareness in meditation, the seeker may enter into the past or the sub-conscious or may become clairvoyant. People may experience such heat if you try to focus your eyes on the Agnya chakra. It would be better to focus on the sahasrar chakra or on the space between the two nostrils where they separate in the respiratory system, as it helps to bring back the body in balance.

Hence it is important that while meditating one should be in a balanced state. If we are trying to strain the left or right sympathetic systems, it will ultimately break the connection with the central path of the parasympathetic. Licentious behavior and its justification through perverted intelligential arguments cannot help us in our evolution but will only expedite destruction of the human personality. Shree Mataji explains that the argument is always put forward that if you inhibit your desires a phenomenon of conditioning takes place. But one must realize that if you indulge in your desires too much, your ego gets conditioned too. The unfortunate part is that the awareness of ego conditioning is not evident. In such cases the ego becomes colossal that the harm caused by the ego conditioning is not evident, and it is even greater that the super-ego conditioning commonly known as sub-conscious suppression. The middle-path is the fulcrum which rests on wisdom.

Knowledge of abnormal people cannot guide the destiny of normal human beings. Licentiousness makes man depraved and weak personalities and finds himself ill-equipped to fulfill the program of evolution that is built-in in him. In conclusion, Shree Mataji says that for a seeker of Sahaja yoga it is necessary to become like a child to enter the kingdom of heaven i.e. the Sahasrara. He must lead a life of temperance, piety and virtue, with respect of familiar and filial relations. Judgment, relying on the artificial behavior of modern times does not depict the deep significance divine love.

The unconscious.

Speaking on the sanctity of marriage and the wonderful benediction that it showers, Shree Mataji says, that at this juncture of Kaliyuga, what is necessary is to provide the spiritual parenthood for the many great souls who are waiting to be re-born to ascend into higher stages of evolution. Hence to move from the four stages of awareness into the fifth dimension we should develop divine discrimination to lead of life of balanced activity, neither of indulgence nor of total abstinence leading to a personality devoid of love and compassion. The Mooladhara chakra emits electromagnetic vibrations which with the tetravalent valency balance the positive or the negative valences of the other elements thereby firmly keeping the personality grounded. If this chakra gets disturbed, a person's discrimination gets affected and is easily influenced by passing fancies and perverted tendencies.

Hence the secret to develop divine discrimination is to maintain the sanctity, innocence and chastity of the Mooladhar chakra that guides the sahaja yogi as a magnet to its goal.

Chapter 6

Likes and dislikes

The beauty and excellence that we see in people, children, creatures, plants, nature, music and even inanimate objects like carpets, are reflections of aspects of our own nature that we acknowledge as beautiful. Flowers, gardens, music, art architecture and other works of beauty, art or excellence that we create, or simply appreciate are all reflections of the beauty or excellence in our own nature.

When we like or dislike what others do or what they stand for, this touches on aspects of our own nature which we are either happy to acknowledge or prefer to ignore. The greater our identification with them, the more intense our responses. When we quarrel with someone, we only try to put across our point of view without listening to someone else's. We become biased and prejudiced in our opinions. This leads to friction and may even get to a point where people don't talk to each other and want to have anything to do with each other.

When we are in a group talking to each other or discussing any common subject, we should respect the other individual's viewpoint and give him a chance to express it without interruption, and then perhaps he will give you the same opportunity. Nothing brings a person of a sound mind to the point of violence more quickly than the feeling that you are not listening to him. Listening indicates respect. Listening makes the other person feel important. Let the person to whom we are talking to know that we can appreciate the way he feels. We can settle earlier misunderstandings or ill feeling by saying, "You must have felt very upset and irritated when the last time you asked me to help you, and I did not. It might have made you feel that I couldn't care less." Or "If the situation was reversed, I would feel the same like you."

We find that we often communicate better with a person who will listen to us without judging. We all need to have at least one person with whom we can open our hearts without having to fear about anything. We all need to be that person who will accept others as they are. Many times there is no need for a listener to express any opinion. Just to be able to be there so that others can share their feelings with a sympathetic human being is enough.

I read a beautiful chapter in Gods and Godmen of India, a book written by Khushwant Singh, where in he narrates an interview with God. I reproduce it here.

I dreamed I had an interview with God. "Come in," God said, "So you would like to interview me?"

"If you have the time." I said. God smiled and said, "My time is eternity and is enough to do everything; what questions do you have in mind to ask me?"

"What surprises you most about mankind?" I asked.

God answered: "That they get bored with being children; are in rush to grow up, and then long to be children again. That they lose their health to make money and then lose their money to restore their health; That by thinking anxiously about their future, they forget the present, such that they live neither for the present nor for the future. That they live as if they will never die and die as if they have never lived..."

God's hands shook and we were silent for a while. Then I asked..."As a parent, what are some of life's lessons you want your children to learn?"

God replied with a smile, "To learn that they cannot make anyone love them: what they can do is to let themselves be loved. To learn that what is most valuable is not what they have in their lives, but who they have in their lives to learn that it is not good to compare themselves to others.

"All will be judged individually on their own merits, not as a group on a comparison basis! To learn that a rich person is not the one who has the most, but is one who needs the least. To learn that it only takes a few seconds to open profound wounds in persons we love and that it takes many years to heal them.

"To learn that there are persons who love them dearly, but simply do not know how to express or show their feelings. To learn that money can buy everything but happiness. To learn that money can buy everything but happiness. To lean that two people can look at the same thing and see it totally differently. To learn that a true friend is someone who knows everything about them…. and likes them anyway. To learn that it is not always enough that they are forgiven by others, but that they have to forgive themselves.

I sat there for a while enjoying the moment. I thanked Him for His time and for all that He has done for me and my family. He replied: "I'm here twenty-four hours a day. All you have to do is to ask for me and I'll answer."

In Her talk at Rahuri in 1987, Shree Mataji's parting words were," You have to be giving like the sun…. You carry the sun with you. And you should spread love and warmth and let them feel that the sun has been brought from India by you.…. You are yogis, you are not ordinary people, and you are Yogis. You · represent that category of people who are known for their righteousness, for their compassion, and love. So I wish you all best of love, enjoy your journey, enjoy everything and pass this joy that you have achieved here to other people, to other Sahaja Yogis and to other people who are not even Sahaja Yogis.

Chapter 7

Giving and Generosity

Giving has the greatest joy and pleasure. As Sahaja yogis all joy giving qualities are within us which we should discover. The more we give to others the more Life will give to us. This involves forgetting our own welfare and being more thoughtful about the needs of others.

After being enlightened in Sahaja yoga we could give our time and devote our energies for the emancipation of human beings by helping them come up in life. Instead of finding faults with them or condemning them we could help them in a positive way by helping them to stabilize themselves in their meditation. We can be channels for the flow of unlimited love which has the power to bind all those who give it to each other. Love is a force that can transform people in a way as to accommodate more people, have a tolerant attitude of the limitations of the other and help them to find their strengths.

The generous appreciation of the loveliness of the good qualities in others, the real caring about the happiness and welfare of others the giving of ourselves and our belongings to those who need it all can be cultivated and made to grow in us. Instead of repressing the feelings and passions within us, if we give it an expression by having a sincere desire for the better, for the lovelier things in life, not only for ourselves, but for all life around us then it is easier to grow in spirituality.

"You are here for your journey alone. And even though you have been provided the comfort of much camaraderie along the way, each of you is, in actuality, flying solo in your "moments of truth."

As it is said, blessed are those who ask nothing of the universe, but only give. The great sage Patanjali said that when all desire to possess ceases, then all things flow to a man's feet. Shri Mataji has said several times, that generosity is the only way you can express your love to others. All your material wealth and everything have no meaning unless you show generosity for other people, but one should do it silently. All the great saints, the Sadhgurus who were born in India were monuments of generosity. Generosity also means to give our time, attention and care to another person. When we fully accept another person by offering forgiveness and tolerance with a generous heart has a tremendous power of healing wounds, feeling of loneliness, fear and insecurity.

Serving another person food before ourselves, helping someone cross the road, assisting a person how to reach a certain place when he feels lost, being willing to listen to a person in distress, allowing others to sit, or pass by are all acts of generosity which involves our attention, loving kindness and sensitivity to a great extent. It is not heroic actions that define generosity but the simple willingness to give and care.

Just being present for someone is one of the greatest acts of generosity and benevolence that one can do for someone. As Shree Mataji said at the Sahasrara Puja at Austria in 1985, When you surrender, you enjoy not only your absoluteness, but you also enjoy seeing that Absoluteness in others. Then in that state of Nirananda your compassion becomes like an ocean to encompass all, and you are willing to give and share with one and all that comes in the sphere of influence.

Chapter 8

Forgiveness

It has been written in all scriptures that one should forgive. Forgiveness is the Divine power under whose vibrations the explosive agitations of anger, guilt and hatred are neutralized. Forgiveness is the strength of the mighty. In today's world where goodness is more often than not, met with opposition, forgiving is the means with which we can release emotionally those who we feel have committed a wrong against us. When we are treated badly, if instead of condemning the offender, we forgive them freely, then we wipe the slate of our consciousness clean. When we forgive someone, we find that some pockets of tension that may have been built somewhere within the body gets released and we find ourselves at peace with ourselves. In the same way, one should also forgive oneself for offences we may have committed so that we can get rid oneself emotionally of the anger that may have built within ourselves.

Why is it sometimes so difficult to forgive and forget that is let go off completely? This is because the human ego demands punishment or vindication for the injustice or wrong done. Feeling "right" by maintaining resentment against others may be more important than forgiving them and enjoying harmony, inner peace and improved health. Insisting on your lawful rights may be more important than the possible benefits of conceding and letting go. This may even mean that there is some satisfaction in maintaining the circumstances as strained as they are. But forgiving is a Divine virtue, hence forgiving someone, will actually make us free of all baggage. Forgiveness involves forgetting, letting go and moving on.

Forgiveness breaks the chain of cause and effect. When someone treats us badly or says something insulting, our response to that action based on anger and resentment builds a wall and affects our relationships. Very often it is not that someone can harm us without our consent, but it is the kind of response based on our pre-conclusions that makes all the difference. It is the consequence of whatever choice we make. This causes more damage than solve problems. As it is said, to err is human but to forgive is divine, every human being makes mistakes so it is better to forgive a person, even before expecting the other person to ask for forgiveness, and focus instead on our own mistakes and make efforts in removing them.

Whenever we are ill we need to introspect and see whom we have not forgiven. Forgiving means giving up, letting go. It has nothing to do with going and telling the person who we feel that we have wronged or who has treated us badly that we have forgiven him or her. It has nothing to do with condoning a certain behavior or action that they have done to us in the past. We do not even have to know how to forgive. All we need to know is to be willing to forgive. We all know how painful it is when we have to undergo the pain and have nobody to understand us. Then we must realize that they who need to be forgiven most, what pain they may be undergoing. We need to understand that what they did at that point of time when they did it, was what best they in their wisdom knew had to be done, the best that they could do with their understanding, awareness and knowledge that they had at that time.

We need to choose to release the past, the burden and baggage of the past by forgiving everyone including ourselves. We need to affirm and say, "I forgive anyone whom I may have hurt by not behaving the way I should have behaved, or the way you wanted me to behave, or the way you wanted me to do it. I forgive you and I set you free." By saying this we become free. And this freedom begins the healing process and we are set on our path for greater enfoldment and expression of our true natural self.

Chapter 9

Trust

When others trust us, they hand us the power that they would not have otherwise given to some one. When some one trusts us, it is our responsibility to see that we do not betray that trust. It is a trust that we shall not harm one another or deceive one another.

When we pass unjust judgments on others, it is because we want to show that we are superior to them in some way. The more inferior we make them appear in our eyes or in the eyes of others the more superior we feel, more so if that person is a socially or politically important or powerful person. We often tend to look for the bad points in other people, regarding their behavior or something what they said, so that we can brand them as useless, or cheap or worthless without considering the circumstances or the situation that have influenced them. It could be that their loneliness, their personal loss or family circumstances that have led to it. Coming to conclusions in this way and labeling them as that kind of man or that kind of woman will only distance ourselves from them and cause disharmony.

We betray the trust of many good people who may be dissimilar to us in many ways but yet their natures may be no less noble than our own.

Don't close your heart even when your feelings have been hurt. For contraction causes its own pain. How others behave towards us is not under our control but how we treat ourselves and we behave towards ourselves when our feelings are hurt is entirely in our hands. We are hurt only when we expect something from another. Quite often we fall a victim to the same expectations even after experiences of earlier failures. This is what hope does to us. Misplaced hope will always cause havoc with the heart until realization. Silent observation and acceptance of our repeated careless responses and misplaced expectations will one day shake our benumbed brain out of its complacency and make us sit up and have a hard look at how we have been reacting. And suddenly all things will click in place.

Divinity works through us in strange ways but our acceptance will make the path a lot easier and lighter.

Chapter 10

Our Growth is our own responsibility

We must realize that every being is here to develop his own evolution according to the dictates of his soul and his Soul alone, and that none of us must do anything except encourage others in that development.

As we grow in Sahaja yoga, it is our growth, our stability, the balance of disposition and the peace and joy that we radiate that will hasten the development of those around us and also attract more people to Sahaja Yoga. Very often, if we try to convert or bring other family members, it can cause much misunderstanding. If someone in the family is following some other path, if we try to put a pressure on that individual into accepting our beliefs, it may not actually work out for that person. Each person must unfold, as each flower, in his or her own time. You cannot force a bud or a seed to become a flower or blossom overnight.

Spirituality is very individual. While we need not and cannot hide and meditate, we should follow our spiritual discipline without making the other family members feel guilty or uncomfortable that they are not doing the same. Otherwise it will only cause resentment.

Shri Mataji has time and again mentioned about the freedom to pursue and bloom in our own freedom and freedom to be wise in our choice. Very often the children who are forced to follow will react by doing exactly the opposite. The best way to attract people and change people is by example, by our own exemplary behavior, by our progress and steady growth, by not thinking that we are superior or trying to show off our spiritual endeavors, but by expressing the kindness, thoughtfulness, love and understanding in very gentle ways, ways that touches people and inspires them to want to know more about the practices that enable you to behave and perform in such an exemplary way.

Chapter 11

Guilt

A sense of guilt at some point of time or the other has caught every one of us. Guilt always looks for punishment and punishment brings pain. When we find a sense of guilt engulfing us, what we should try to do is find out whether it is a factual guilt or you are just feeling guilty without any valid justification for it. This can be done only through a detached, honest and objective analysis and reasoning.

We should check whether we have actually breached any of society's codes or failed to observe any duty or simply because others say that you are guilty. If it is the latter, then they may be expressing opinions that they have themselves adopted from others or it could be factual. If it is factual, then they way to get rid of this guilt is by eliminating the self-destructive messages that we have been feeding ourselves.

If we have set up some or the other mechanisms for our selves that are designed to deprive ourselves they should be eliminated so that we are free to enjoy our true worth, the lead a more fulfilled, respectful and happier life.

This in turn will open the way for the development of the highest aspects of our nature and the fullest expression of our inner beauty and love.

A person who is habituated to feeling guilty will often be found saying, " I knew such a bad thing was going to happen, and you won't be there to help", or "I just thought as much, just when the deadline was approaching, you would go on leave.". Such a person is often the self-pitying kind and would almost invariably draw us into a conversation of how hopeless things are.

Almost always we are pulled off balance, and our energy is drawn into their guilt feeling by creating a doubt on our part. And as soon our energy is drawn into their field of experience, they immediately get a boost of energy and feel more secure.

Guilt and self-pity is also a kind of conditioning which a person has developed over a period of time to meet his need for sympathy or nurturing that he has lacked since childhood or for a long time. When we lend our sympathies to such a person who has been helplessly trapped unknowingly vicious circle of self-validating guilt, we are indirectly energizing the very sentiments and further pushing him into the intimidating traps.

Of course, there will be cases where we should feel concern or sympathy for someone in a difficult situation, but we are not really helping a person by lending our energies that are only boosting a person's guilt trip. When we really and truly practice Sahaja yoga meditation, we develop that state of clarity when in an instant we can recognize self-pity or a genuine difficult situation.

When in the light of our full awareness we respond in a

way so as to present to the person who is on a guilt trip, his unconsciousness will be beaten up to awakening. This can be done with very gentle and polite words such as, "The way you are putting, and it feels to me as if I am supposed to feel guilty for it." Or one could say, "I don't feel that I have done anything wrong at all."

Of course, in such situations we must really have all the courage to say so, because while we are honestly trying to sort out the situation, the other person's reaction would invariably be, "I knew I couldn't count on you for help." On most occasions, the person with the guilt would invariably feel insulted and angry.

In such cases, an enlightened Sahaja yogi is like a mentor to another and is trying to help other to become aware of the state of unconsciousness in which he is in. For this, he has to keep providing the energy and keep the conversation or dialogue going even though he may be at the receiving end of all abuses or insults, as a result of the anger and out burst of the victim of guilt. But eventually, the very act of listening to the outburst will make that person aware of the guilt trip on which he has been riding.

His behavior comes within the light of his own awareness and that light itself is enough to wash away the pain of guilt that he has been harboring all along.

And when he basks in the light of that wisdom, the lightness of feeling that engulfs him as a result of the lifting of a lifetime of guilt will make him truly feel a huge sense of gratitude of having been there for him.

"As long as you cling to the idea of the way "life is supposed to be," your life circumstances will continue to reflect a perspective that sees itself at the effect of circumstances beyond your control."

This is the role a Sahaja yogi has to play dispassionately, in helping one another grow into full bloom, into a fresh new perspective that is refreshingly more nourishing.

Chapter 12

Criticism

How often we have observed people talk ill about others. Talking about the bad qualities of others, gossip and spreading discomforts of our own brothers and sisters begets those very qualities to multiply in us.

Jesus said to one of his disciples, "If one of your brethren was asleep and the wind had blown off his garment, what would you do?"

He answered, "We would cover him."

He said, "No, you would rather expose him further."

They cried, "God forbid that we should act in such a way!"

Jesus said, "But it is the same when you hear a word against your brother and carry it to others!"

Shri Mataji says, don't accept anything bad. Once you start believing a person as bad, a fortress is built and you don't believe anything else. This can be broken open only through Sahaja yoga, when the Brahmarandra, which is the seat of the heart, is opened by the rising kundalini. By raising the kundalini again and again and making the Brahmarandra wider and wider, the heart will take charge of the brain.

The world is like a mirror. Most of the problems we have with people are reflections of the problems we have with ourselves. We don't have to go out and change everyone else. When we gently change some of our own ideas, our relationships improve automatically.

Criticism is destructive. It is the fastest way to create resentment and destroy a relationship. The immediate reaction to criticism is to justify, to blame. It is very easy to say others are wrong but we must realize that we can only correct where we are wrong so what should be easier and more logical is to correct ourselves than to correct others.

If we find faults with one another, if we criticize one another, we are only reducing the energy in the channels which is the power of Sahaja Yoga.

Sahaja yoga is a collective phenomenon; it can work best when all the channels work together in harmony. When collectivity is disturbed through criticism, problems develop in the Vishuddhi whose effect is seen at the Sahasrara where there is an integration of all energies, all powers. All the centers are in the brain, in the Sahasrara. When the brain becomes affected and this goes beyond a certain level, the Heart chakra gets affected. This combination of Vishuddhi, Sahasrara and Heart chakra can be a very deadly combination and if either left or right Agnya joins in, Shri Mataji warns, you develop the Ekadashi Rudra.

Thus criticism in any manner either others of ourselves, locks us in the very same pattern or conditioning that we are trying to come out of. Criticizing has become a habit with most of us and it has never worked. Let us come out of it and see what happens. Understanding and being gentle with ourselves will help us to come out of it. We have to accept ourselves as we are. Self-acceptance and self approval will help us change the pattern and make us more loving towards ourselves and thereby to each other as our Mother has always wanted us to be. Only when compassion starts flowing from us that our channels will become empty to receive more compassion and love from our Mother.

Chapter 13

Creating positive patterns of thought and behavior

When the brain becomes enlightened through regular practice of Sahaja yoga meditation and becoming established in thoughtless awareness and doubtless awareness we can very easily recognize in a witness state our patterns of behavior and consciously make an effort to change into desirable patterns of behavior. In order to be able to do this one must first recognize and acknowledge fearlessly, the lower and the higher, the good and the bad qualities in us. And then slowly, every time the lower aspect of us comes to the front and expresses or tries to express it, the same should be replaced by the higher aspect. It is difficult, no doubt, but it can be done, by persistent efforts, day in and day out. It requires tremendous patience and solid desire to transform into a beautiful human being.

Now, what is it that prevents us from expressing the higher and more sublime qualities is the limiting pattern that we ourselves have cultivated to survive in difficult times, or to attract love or respect that we desired desperately to have.

Let us look at the following behavior patterns:

1. I have to appear to be rich, strong and

intelligent; otherwise I will not have the respect and adoration from people.

2. If I am not respected or admired, I feel unimportant and worthless.

3. I want to appear superior and saintly so as to gain the approval and acceptance of the society.

4. I prefer to be aggressive, critical, rebellious and stubborn as otherwise I feel vulnerable, powerless and controlled.

5. I want to be possessive as otherwise I feel rejected and neglected.

6. I prefer to be unemotional and unavailable as then it gives me a sense of importance and pride of appearing to be busy and in control.

7. I have to appear miserable, angry, helpless, lonely or unwell, if I have to attract sympathy and love.

8. I like to appear independent and desirable as it gives me security, admiration and a sense of being powerful.

9. If I appear to be wise and right, I can attract trust, security and submission of people. Being obeyed, accepted and looked up to is more important to me than being compassionate, caring, loving and responsible.

10. A paternal or a maternal or a dominating demeanor makes me feel included and loved and this is more important to me than being natural, dignified, sincere and honest.

11. I try to conform to what is normal in the society as I do not want to be unloved, excluded, unwanted or rejected if I try to be different.

When we observe these patterns what we need to do is prevent ourselves from expressing it the next time. Our brain is a highly sensitive and sophisticated instrument. It is easy to lower the standards of integrity by mentally justifying that if we do not behave that way people will take advantage of us. It is easy to succumb to patterns of paralyzing behavior. We need to constantly remind ourselves that we have to cultivate the higher aspects as this will give us greater fulfillment in life. The change has to happen slowly. Hasten slowly as it is said. Perseverance is the key word. If at any point of time we find ourselves saying or doing something we had decided to throw out of our system, do not be angry or annoyed with yourself. Forgive yourself. Make a greater resolve not to repeat the next time that happens.

"There is no place in the transcendent consciousness for any of the baggage you may still be carrying. All the shoulds and shouldn'ts that may have dominated your consciousness, are to be released and left at this crossroads."

In due course of time, the realigned pattern of behavior will start showing results. The limiting or crippling behavior patterns will fade and disappear and there will come a time when we ourselves will wonder, whether we were like that. The gradual change will bring out the finest qualities and the innermost beauty will shine in exuberance.

Love manifests in our courtesies towards all, particularly those who we do not know. When we do something for others, it may be because subconsciously it may be the same thing what we wish to be done to us in similar situations.

It can be seen in our identification with others even those with whom we are in conflict, seeing in their behavior, their hopes, fears and needs and recognizing them to be no different from our own. It rejoices in wishing the welfare of others just as it would have been if it was for our own fulfillment.

In the course of a conversation, listen to the other person respectfully. Irritated people are usually surprised when you ask, "Is there anything else you want to tell me?" They are so used to listening the other person asking them to shut up, that when you ask them so beautifully, all their aggression will evaporate and will start behaving very sweetly.

Often the problem is not that we don't care, but we do not know how to show or express that we do care. One way would be to give our total attention when someone is talking to us. It is listening with a sense of deep receptivity. When we are deeply receptive, then in that mindful stillness, in the absence of formulation of response, in the absence of an impatience to interject when the other person is speaking, there is more than a mere exchange of words. In those moments are possibilities of connection at a deeper level, moments that can be charged with awareness, moments that can give us a chance to select the words that we speak, words that are nice, sweet words, not words that would wound.

The awareness holds the potential to be a source of connectedness that can build bonds of love with all people who come in contact with us. Our communication is non-judgmental, non-reactive but holds a cultivated restraint.

Chapter 14

Intuition and vibratory awareness

The discretion of the Ida Nadi is intuition. If we develop that discretion within through our meditative powers, we develop intuition. Intuition is nothing but taking the help of the Ganas, who are surrounding all sahaja yogis. If we learn to take help from the Ganas without much difficulty we tend to say the right thing. The whole of Sahaja Yoga, Shri Mataji says, say fifty percent at least out of that, is based on intuition.

What is intuition? How does it work?

Intuition is a perception beyond the physical senses that assists us in all fronts. It is the new awareness that arises once the Kundalini is awakened, and the whole central nervous system is enlightened, and which allows us to feel what is happening to the chakras of ourselves and those of others. If we can accept that every atom possesses a form of consciousness, then when atoms of like consciousness come together and coalesce, there comes into existence a body of energy which expresses a definite vibratory pattern. These energy patterns are present in the form of the seven major chakras in the human being. Each major charka is associated with a different frequency and quality of energy. But consciousness as an energy field is something that is extra sensory and is able to operate beyond the limitations of space and time.

Collective consciousness is the ability that emerges when we are able to raise our awareness above the level of individual egos and merge our energy fields and be able to work interactively with others. For example when Gene Rodenberry imagined a future where Star Trek's Spock was able to meld his mind with others, we find that more of us are able to intuitively read others' thoughts and emotions and also able to think and create together without having to consciously communicate through our five senses.

We have to reach that absolute point where we can jump into collective consciousness. It is beyond thinking and can be felt on the fingers. They are the signal that comes from the Absolute and that has to be decoded through Nirmal Vidya that Shri Mataji has so lovingly been teaching us all these years. The Kundalini records and decodes all that information and tells us from time to time what is right and what is wrong. It is in the fullest of awareness that we come to know, not only about others but about the whole.

When the Kundalini rises, our attention or awareness is filled with enlightenment. In that state of consciousness, our subtle system has the ability to understand itself, control it and be connected to the all pervading vibratory fields. Hence even when we are not thinking, by merely being thoughtlessly aware, our operating system can feel on the finger tips and hands the cool breeze about the energy centers of others and will be able to control the relationship with others.

This consciousness which is present in each and every person, in the form of vibrations, on being awakened

61

can be used intelligently to improve our present situation and in general help the whole mankind to go to a higher level.

WHAT WE CAN DO WITH VIBRATIONS?
(Source - www.valaya.co.uk)

Vibrations are a very useful extra sense. It is the element of the Sahasrara Chakra, the centre of integration whose nature is Absolute Truth. By feeling Vibrations we can know the truth in many ways. We can know the state of our own being, whether we are getting sucked into any illusions or troubled by thoughts, worries or even desires. We can check the Vibrations of anyone alive or dead, anywhere in the world, and we can work on them by giving bandhans. Strong cool vibrations indicate that the person is or were a realized soul. We can check the Vibrations of any thing, such as books, films, artifacts etc... It is not necessary to read a book or see a film or painting to get an idea of its Vibrations and hence the sort of effect it might have on us.

We can even ascertain the vibrational outcome of any decision that we may be going to take. By asking to be shown the Vibrations of different outcomes one can get a clearer idea of what are good decisions spiritually. For example if one was having a difficult time at work, one might ask the questions: Should I stay working here? , and Would it be better to leave?, One of these alternatives might feel cooler on the hands, with less catches; we might also feel our attention rise up to Sahasrara and enter a state of thoughtlessness for one and come down to Agnya or lower for the other. One may also feel the Spirit in the heart jump with joy for one alternative, and another way of sensing is to put attention on the Void (abdomen); a good decision will feel comfortable, calm and grounded, and a worse one fluttery.

We can use vibrations to check the truth of any concept or thought, to find out whether they are genuine or not. For example, one can ask questions like: Is there God?, Who is Shri Mataji?, Can we save people from the grip of materialism?, A flow of cool Vibrations and a state of thoughtlessness and bliss as the attention rises to Sahasrara indicates Truth. We can also ask to be shown the truth of any facts (2+2=4 has vibrations, 2+2=7 not so much) or situations (Was this person responsible for this act?)

However, we should be careful while checking the Vibrations of things or situations where in we are emotionally involved, as we can be fooled. In such situations it is probably wise to ask a disinterested person to check for us. A way of checking things without any bias is to write the alternatives on pieces of paper, mix them up so we don't know which is which, and test the Vibrations of the different pieces of paper.

Chapter 15

Purity of Dedication to your Goal

The great Sufi saint Rumi, says that Love is the factor that will carry a man, in fact all humanity to fulfillment. "Mankind has an unfulfilled desire and he struggles to fulfill it through all kinds of enterprises and ambitions. But it is only love that he can find fulfillment." But love itself is something which goes hand in hand with enlightenment. Both increase together.

Enlightenment of the brain gives us all the subtle understanding of the all pervading cosmic power. After kundalini awakening one often experiences blissful happenings, miraculous coincidences and situations that appeared so difficult before being done in such a facile manner. It often makes us wonder, what is it that has made things happen? How is it that I got this blessing? How could these transformations take place? When the brain starts understanding these wonderful happenings, it starts trusting the heart.

When the brain starts trusting the heart, devotion arises within us and it becomes totally surrendered to the Brahmarandra which is the seat of the heart. Now it is the liver that is controlled by the Swadishthan chakra that supplies energy or fuel to the brain to think. But when the brain becomes surrendered to the heart, all thinking comes from the Swadishthan which is the seat of all creativity. Hence all work done by the brain becomes enlightened work. The brain which is enlightened and connected to the all pervading power, when it works on creative ideas, it achieves results. Thus an enlightened person has the power to achieve anything.

An enlightened person, whose kundalini is awakened and linked to the cosmic power around, he becomes an instrument of Divine force. Thus, when the Atma tattwa is awakened, the light of wisdom shines forth through the intellect and his mind emits a fragrance of love unblemished by the egoistic desires. Such a person is accommodative and can truly influence the collective consciousness.

The Sahasrar chakra is the final development of the subtle system within humans, enabling to rise, in every sense, above the world of mental activity and emotional concepts. The collective consciousness which arises when the Kundalini energy rises through the Sahasrar chakra allows direct perception of reality on the central nervous system. We can know ourselves as pure spirit, pure joy, pure attention and pure truth. Vibratory awareness allows our perception to transcend the senses and go to the essence of all creation.

Shree Mataji speaks of the 14 stages of reaching the Sahasrar chakra in Her speech on the Mahasahasrar Puja on 5th May, 1984, excerpt of which are given below.

"Fourteen years ago (or we could say already thirteen years have passed and now the fourteenth year has started) this great work of opening the Sahasrara was accomplished in this world. I have told you about this many times on every Sahasrara day; as to what had happened, how it was done and what its importance is. But the fourteenth birthday is very important because man lives at fourteen levels and the day he crosses over the fourteenth level, he becomes a complete Sahaja Yogi. Therefore, today Sahaja Yoga has also become Sahaja Yogi.

God has created fourteen levels within us. If you simply count them, then you know that there are seven Chakras within us. Besides these, there are two more Chakras, about which you do not talk much-they are the chakra of Moon (Lalita) & chakra of Sun (Shri). Then there is "Hamsa" Chakra. Thus there are three more-seven plus three make ten. Then-there are four chakras above the Sahasrara. And about these chakras also, I have told you-ARDHA-BINDU, BINDU, VALAYA and PRADAKSHINA. These are the four.

After coming to Sahaja Yoga and after your Sahasrara has opened, you have to pass through these four chakras, ARDHA-BINDU, BINDU, VALAYA and PRADAKSHINA. After passing through these four chakras only, can you say that you have become a Sahaja Yogi. And if you see from another angle, we have to cross fourteen stages in reaching up to Sahasrara; if you divide them then there are seven chakras situated on Ida Nadi (Channel) and seven on Pingla Nadi.

When man makes his ascent, he does not do so in straight direction. He comes first to left then goes to right, then again to left and then again to right.

And when Kundalini ascends, it also does so, dividing Herself into these two. The reason for it can be understood if I take the example of two ropes. These two ropes together, side by side-in the process of going up or coming down cross over twice. When Kundalini ascends, you see on the chakra whether the left in caught or the right is caught. Although Kundalini is only one, but on every chakra you see both the things-thus you know whether left is caught or the right. Thus, within us, if each chakra is divided into these two-left and right---then seven two's are, fourteen; similarly within us first of all fourteen stages have to be crossed before reaching the Sahasrara. And if you understand this-that these seven, and seven above-this way also a path of fourteen is created.

Therefore this thing 'fourteen' is very important in Kundalini Shastra (Science). We should fully under-stand that we become entitled to the Blessings of Sahaja Yoga only after rising above these fourteen stages. We should unceasingly march forward and (as we imbibe it) get completely 'dyed' in it.

Rajana, Birajana-these words I have said to you many times earlier, also; but today, specially, we should understand that on Sahasrara day what is Rajana (to reign, to be the master), what is Birajana (to assume).

Now, you are sitting, you look at these trees. This is the tree of Shriphala. Coconut is called Shriphala. This grows along the sea-coast. The best fruit grows at the sea coast-the reason is, the sea-it is the 'Dharma'. Wherever there is dharma, only there, the Shriphala blossoms. Where there is no dharma, Shriphala will not grow there.

All things are contained in the sea. All sorts of-cleanliness, dirt; everything is inside it. This water is also full of salt. Christ had said that 'You are the salt of the earth'. Means, you can enter into everything. You can impart taste to everything. The 'prana-shakti' (Life-force) that we take in, if we don't have salt within us, then even that pranashakti cannot work. it is a catalyst. And this salt-it fully organises for us to live, to live in this world, to live in the 'prapancha' (illusionary world).

But when this thing rises towards God (Paramatma), then it leaves all the salt below -everything is left. And when the light of the sun falls on these trees, the sap of the whole tree is sucked upwards – through its leaves because evaporation takes place-then, this water flows upwards through the trunk;--leaving 'everything'. It crosses those fourteen things and on reaching the top, is formed Shriphala. You are that same Shriphala.

Also Shriphala is made up in a strange way, There is no 'phala' (fruit) in the world like the Shriphala. No part of it (tree) goes waste. You can see that the Shriphala is also like human being's Sahasrara. Like the hair we have, the same way Shriphala also has hair. You are protected by them. And inside this-like we have cranial bones- inside the Shriphala too there's a hard kind of a covering on the outside. After that inside us--- grey matter and white matter-two such things are inside us. In the Shriphala, too, you see-white matter and grey matter,... and inside that is water, which is the cerebrospinal fluid inside us. Inside that (Shriphala) also there is water-that is the limbic area.

Our brain is the fruit of the whole of our evolution. Through this brain we have got all kinds of powers. With this is collected all the wealth that has been received by us. Now, the Atma (Spirit) resides inside this heart and after Sahaja-Yoga its light spreads within us in seven layers, from both sides that can happen only when one's Sahasrara is open.

Till now, we have been doing the same job with our brain -ego and super-ego-- But after realization, we work with the help of our Atma. Atma, before realization resides within the heart,--absolutely separate-as a 'Kshetragya'(witness of the field). It is separate from us. It is not in our Chitta. After realization, it comes into our Chitta, first which you know, is in the Void. After that, its light comes into the truth, because as the brain gets enlightened we know the truth. "Know". Doesn't mean that we know through the intellect, but know in reality (Sakshat) that this is the truth'. After that its light is seen in the heart. The heart becomes profound, heart starts expanding, starts becoming vast, its power of love starts increasing. That's why-'Sacchidananda-Sat, Chitta and Anand (Truth, attention and bliss (joy). Truth within our brain, Chitta, within our dharma; and joy within our Atma-start getting enlightened. Its light spreads gradually at first. It's a subtle thing, and in the gross set-up we live in, it becomes difficult to catch hold of that subtle. Gradually that hold also develops, After that you start to grow, to progress. With the opening of a single curtain of Sahasrara, the Kundalini comes up. But its light does not start spreading all around just then. The Kundalini has just come up and you have saluted the seat of Sadashiva. Within you, the light of Atma has started flowing hazily. But it has not yet fully blossomed in this brain.

Now, the surprising thing is, that if you want to spread it through your brain, you cannot. You know well, that when you work too much with your intellect, heart-failure occurs. And when you work too much with your heart, the brain fails. There exists a relationship between them. It's a very deep relationship. And because of this deep relationship, when you get your realisation their relationship has to become deeper. The moment it gets completely integrated, your (Chitta) attention becomes completely Parameshwar-Swarup, (one with supreme God).

But how can the dissolution of ego and super-ego are effected ? If you beat down the ego, the super-ego comes up, if you beat down the super-ego, the ego comes up. How to win over the super-ego and the ego? There's only one door for that-Agnya chakra. By working on the Agnya-chakra the two, get completely dissolved, And as soon as they get dissolved, the heart and brain first establish a complete concord. "it is this oneness that we have to achieve."

So, your heart becomes the Sahasrara and your Sahasrara, the heart. What you think is in your heart; and whatever is in your heart, that only you think. When your state becomes like this, then, any kind of doubts, any kind of disbelief, any kind of fear-no such thing remains. When both the things become one you try to understand this point-which the brain, through which you think, makes your Manas understand, and takes care of it; that brain it becomes your Mana. When such a state comes, then you become the complete Master (Guru). Such a state we should definitely achieve.

Definitely, you have become Shriphala. But I always talk of what is ahead. Have you seen how people climb the coconut tree? He ties a rope around himself and keeps hooking that rope higher and with its help, he climbs. In the same way, as we climb, our own rope has always to be kept hooked higher. Only then your climbing is very quick. But mostly we keep hooking the rope lower. While coming down, you do not even need to hook the rope. You just loosen it a bit and-zoom -you will come down ! That arrangement is already made-for coming down. It is to climb up, for which arrangement has to be made. So, to become something, hard work has to be put in.

Therefore 'Always set your sight higher' Now even to see this fruit (Shriphala), you have to take your sight up. Even their sight is set upwards, because without keeping their sight upwards,-they know- that 'neither can they get Surya or get this work done, nor can they, become Shriphala.

Your Sahasrara is also like this very Shriphala-is extremely dear to Mother ; and this very Sahasrara should be surrendered to Her. And the One, who is sitting there, 'is the 'fruit' of 'all' things. The roots of this tree, fixed in the soil below, they are also borne out from It. Its trunk, its hard work, its evolution - all' this in the end becomes that fruit. Everything is inherent in that fruit. You put that fruit in the soil and again the whole of this thing will be borne out.

In the whole world, whatever work of God has taken place, the form of its fruit is our Mahayoga of today! So you should feel blessed and becoming like this "Shriphala", you should be surrendered in offering. It is only removed from the tree when it is mature-otherwise it is useless. If it is removed from the tree and then offered, only then is the Puja considered accomplished. So, to understand Sahaja Yoga,--in a very great symbolic-form verify (Sakshat) Shriphala itself is standing before you.

In the same way you also have Shriphala. Fully mature it. There is only one way to mature it, that you have concord with your heart. There is no difference between the heart and the brain. From the heart we desire and from the brain it is fulfilled. When both the things become one, only then will you be fully benefited. You have got it for a very much higher purpose and keep it at that higher level and only on attaining that accomplished wonderful unique state you can consider yourself blessed.

Look at these trees. The breeze is flowing in the opposite direction. Actually the trees should be bent towards this side. But in which direction are the trees bowing down ? Have you ever marked that all the trees are facing in that direction ? Why ? The breeze is coming from that direction and pushing them, even then, why are the trees bending towards the same side ? Because they know that 'It' (Sea) is the one who is the Giver of everything. Being reverent and extremely humble, (;")they are bowing to It. The dharma which is inside us, when it gets fully awakened, starts fully manifesting, only then will the Shriphala inside us be so sweet, beautiful and nourishing. And then the world will get to know from your life itself-'what you are'-and not from anything else.

To accept any kind of compromise, to loosen hold on yourself in any matter, does not behove a Sahaja Yogi. A person who is a Sahaja Yogi, should bravely make his path and move forward. Look at the way these trees hold such a heavy fruit so high. In the same way you have to hold your head high and while holding it high, remember that the head should be respectfully bowed towards the sea-the sea, which is the sign of dharma. It has to be reverently and humbly bowed (;) towards the Dharma.

Finally, the brain, or the Sahasrara should radiate love .We should only consider whether-"Whatever I am doing, is it in love ? Is everything, my talking and all my activities being done in love ?" And if you are really doing that then you have accomplished and acquired that thing, about which I have been speaking, namely "that concord" which should be achieved. So that concord has been established within you. There is only one Shakti (power) which we may call 'Love' and it is only 'Love' that shapes all things to become beautiful, shapely and fully organised. (Anant Ashirvad) to you all.

Chapter 16

Stress Management through Sahaja   Yoga

Man today finds himself in a very unique situation of having to respond and tackle a variety of complex situations day in and day out for which he finds even his multi-dimensional personality inadequate. Ours is a restless age- an age where rapid changes in technology are causing a breakdown of old values and fragmenting our personality. The result of this is tremendous psychological disturbances, stress and tension. Happiness seems to be eluding us and we are constantly seeking answers. In the name of religion people of different countries and communities are waging a war amongst themselves.

Self-realization is the only way you can get the light in.

Sahaja Yoga is a simple technique of self-realization, wherein the dormant energy, which is inborn within you, is awakened and connected with the all-pervading cosmic energy. It is an empirically verifiable scientific method that explains how the very desire for becoming united with the Absolute is built within us as Kundalini.

What is Stress?
Stress is anything that causes fear, anxiety, worry, apprehensions, anger and even excitement when we face difficult situations in daily life, whether mental

or emotional. Continuous efforts to cope with such situations have adverse effects on human systems for want of relief from mental and emotional strains and it leads to diseases. According to Dr. Vernon Coleman, who after discussions with several doctors from various regions, has come to the conclusion that 90-95% of the illnesses can be blamed totally or mainly on psychological forces, 98% headaches are stress or pressure-related, a vast majority of indigestions are due to stress etc.

Some stress is good and even found necessary to feel stimulated, to keep away from boredom and depression and to achieve improved performance. A sense of high achievements and high self-esteem enables a person to cope with higher and higher levels of stress till the optimum level or stress threshold is reached.

What is Stress threshold?
Stress threshold is the point where any more pressure will become counter productive. It is the point where more pressure will lead to fall in productivity and contentment. This point differs from person to person, depending upon one's ability to cope with the pressure. Some people can sustain higher levels of pressure; some thrive on stress while some suffer enormously even under modest amounts of stress. There are fairly fixed stress threshold levels for activity and inactivity. At one end there is inactivity that we can cope with and at the other end, it is activity that we can cope with. If the range between them is narrow one is stress-prone.

When Stress is harmful?
By itself stress never causes a problem. It is the way

one responds to stress which leads to problems. The response is generally in three stages:

Alarm - In the face of a challenge or a threat, the nervous system is highly stimulated, heart rate increases, muscles become tense, and breathing becomes fast. The body system is now ready to fight or flee.

Resistance - If the cause producing the stress continues the body chemistry adjust to that situation (i.e. steady flow of adrenal and other glands secretion and in order to keep the body at a more easily maintained level of arousal during the time needed to fight or get away.

Exhaustion - If the challenge continues for a long time, the resources for arousal and resistance are used. They are involuntary physical responses to stress for which built-in mechanisms exists in the human body. Even imagining or thinking about an upcoming situation may trigger these.

So long as the problem is solved and we are able to rest, even the acute effects of stress are not dangerous to a healthy person. Due to repeated occurrences of emergencies, the person has to pass through the stages of alarm and resistance time and again in the accumulated pressures causing exhaustion, diseases or emotional problems, leading to fall in performance levels, productivity and strained relations within the family and at workplace. Some times, however, a person may even get withdrawn into a depression. These are chronic effects of stress, which are the signals that life style or work habits should be adjusted before worst problems emerge. Hence the importance of effective stress management.

Stress Management

A number of ways have been evolved over the years to tackle stress. Many resort to drinking, smoking, and drugs etc., which are harmful. Relaxation techniques have been found to be more effective than others and meditation is the best relaxation technique. In Sahaja yoga, the regular practice of meditation, after the self-realization, can bring necessary additional change as the person is evolved leading to a balanced outlook toward events and situations he has to face in daily life.

Stress Management through Sahaja Yoga -
Sahaja yoga meditation brings about equilibrium between the sympathetic and Para-sympathetic nervous system response in the process knocking down the sympathetic dominance usually seen in stressful situations, and thereby helps prevent stress disorders.

The technique is simple- it is a way of activating a mechanism- the kundalini- which is the divine energy that lies dormant at the base of the spine. This mechanism is the moving force of our enlightenment and is a living force, which seeks self-organization, self-regeneration and ascent. Through self-organization it sustains and protects the human system. Self-regeneration is its innate ability to heal, renew, balance and recycle. And, ascent is its ability to transcend the mind and body and to attain collective consciousness.

One who practices Sahaja Yoga meditation, finds himself move into a different dimension which enables him to harness the unused sectors of the brain. Once this happens, a new supply of energy is available to us. The actual experiences of people moving into this level of functioning are a feeling of total inner silence, complete health and well-being. There is thoughtless awareness and the person feels a cool breeze of vibrations on the head and on the palms of the hands.

Recent research conducted on varied groups of individual Sahaja Yoga meditators has revealed that the practice of Sahaja Yoga is accompanied by decrease in tension, anxiety, depression, neuroticism and hypertension. With meditation there is an experience of inner peace and harmony and one move in the direction of greater self-control, self-awareness, actualizing one potential and thus moving towards happiness.

Electrical Brain Activity-
Electroencephalograph (EEG) reports indicate the following changes in the brain activity during Sahaja Yoga meditation:

1. At the initial stage, on commencing meditation, the alpha brain wave pattern increases, which creates a sense of relaxed awareness?

2. As the meditation progresses the brain activity shifts to long chains of low voltage theta activity signifying deep physiological relaxation as is attained during deep sleep states.

3. And, during a very deep meditation state, the EEG pattern again changes and this time bursts of high efficiency beta peaks occur.

It appears from all these studies conducted that the human nervous system begins to function in an entirely different way after the Sahaja Yoga meditation practice. Some other dramatic changes clearly reported are:

1. Oxygen consumption decreases within 5 minutes of starting the meditation.

2. Heart rate and respiration rate also decrease.

3. Blood lactate concentration, which is associated with high states of anxiety, also reduces.

4. Adrenalin, which correlates with high blood pressure, drops.

5. The galvanic skin response is a measure of the activity of the sweat glands. This is related to the sympathetic nervous system that regulates the level of tension or relaxation. The Sahaja Yoga practice increases skin resistance thereby significantly reducing tension.

Dr. D Chugh at the Lady Harding Hospital, New Delhi, has conducted these experimental studies.

Chapter 17

Sahaja Yoga and Management

Management is an exceedingly complex art. It is at times mathematics, at times poetry, but always in balanced sense. Management means dealing with people. It is the responsibility of the managers to get the maximum out of the people for the maximum productivity. For the managers have to understand human nature and behavior. So the first step towards management will be to know what the qualities of good manager are and then how to transform the human beings for the best results of the Organization.

QUALITY OF A GOOD MANAGER:

- He by nature is not resistant to organizational needs and normally considers work as a natural activity.

- He is ready and eager to assume responsibility.

- He has no favorites.

- He is not rude, irritable, hard-driving and rough manager on the other hand believes that good relations increase productivity.

- He has no immoral behavior to his colleagues of opposite sex.

- He is creative.

- He is lovable.

- He is not adverse to change in an organization

Man's desires are unlimited. As soon as one is fulfilled, another appears in its place. Once a need is satisfied it no longer becomes a motivator of action and behavior. When the physiological needs of man such as food, clothing and shelter are reasonable satisfied, his next need is safety that means security of employment and freedom of arbitrary management actions. When physiological and security needs are satisfied, his social needs become important. He wants to have a feeling of belonging, a sense of being part of a social group or community. The next need of man after all this is his need for achievement – the gratification of ego and self-importance . In this way the desires keep increasing to aggrandizement and accumulation. There is a lack of satisfaction which ultimately will have behavioral consequences.

Learning is not believing.
The Japanese believe that continuous training can lead to continuous improvement in performance. Therefore, in most Japanese Companies, everyone from Sweeper to a Managing Director attends training classes throughout their career. This approach is also known as the Zen approach, as opposed to the Chinese approach, which is known as Confucius approach. According to the Zen approach, the purpose of training is continuous improvement in the performance of whatever one does- no matter what one's work is, everyone can improve on his or her career by continuous training. The Confucius approach, on the other hand, holds that the aim of training is to qualify the trainee for a more important

job, in other words, the training is for promotion. The Confucius approach emphasizes attention to status, wages and other benefits, rather than the excellence of work.

Today management experts are talking and lecturing on TQM (Total Quality Management), Zero Defect Management etc. The mantra of continuous improvement like other TQM Principles sounds wonderful. But it is not easy to implement. So, while the management commitment to continuous improvement may be unflinching, it is often unable to translate the noble intention into action. It may be noticed that these are all a mental approach. These management experts are overlooking the fundamental fact that humans being can not be transformed into better humans only by learning and training.

When a human mind is exposed to certain knowledge or behavioral attitude only through the mental approach, the process of learning and training, up to a certain point is absorbed but after that it coils back. It generates reactions in his mind, body and life style. Thus after some time, the manager and executives may not be able to contribute their best by training alone

TRANSFORMATION IS AN INSIDE JOB:

According to the Meta Science of Sahaja Yoga, as revealed by H H Mataji Nirmala Devi. H. Shri Mataji Nirmala Devi, there exists a subtle system in each human being, consisting of various energy centers called chakras and nadis or nervous system which control our physical, mental and spiritual activities. They manifest in gross body outside the spinal cord and neural plexuses and control functions of respective parts of the human body. The nadis can be further classified as the central nervous system and the autonomous nervous system.

The autonomic nervous system consists of the parasympathetic and sympathetic nervous system. The sympathetic nervous system is further subdivided into left and right. The LSNS(left sympathetic nervous system) which is also called Ida nadi or moon channel represents the power of desire in individual. It brings our attention to memories of the past. The energy flow in the nadi is blocked by conditioning, superstitions, guilt feelings, too much self-pity, sexual perversion and pornography. Movement in this side gives rise to reactions, which are stored in a balloon like structure on the right side of the brain known as superego. As long as this channel is active there is a human desire to remain alive.

RSNS (right sympathetic nervous system) represents our power of actions. It is also known as pingala nadi or sun channel. It makes us to think, work, plan and organize for the future events. The reactions generated due to all these actions are stored in a balloon like structure at the end of this channel at the left side of the brain and is known as ego.

While we may have control over sympathetic nervous system, it consumes a lot of our energy.

Thus the managers or people who are using LSNS too much are people who
- Often think of the past, are very emotional, avoid meeting people and are introverts.

- They cannot face criticism.
- Such managers are by nature indolent and work little, lack ambition, and dislike responsibilities.
- They are inherently self centered and indifferent to organizational needs.
- They prefer to be led.
- They are by nature resistant to change.
- They are gullible and ready dupe of the charlatans and the demagogue.
- They sit in the corner of the office and try to hide themselves.
- Efforts of the management fail to obtain the desired improvement
- In these types of people as there is no harmony which results in poor performance.
- In other words, these groups of people are dealt with management by control and this does not yield optimum result.

The managers or people who are using there RSNS are:

- Always very aggressive.
- They like to dominate over others and make employees or colleague's life miserable.
- If they are leaders or head of the departments, they do not delegate anything so as to keep the credit of any success for themselves only.
- They become barrier for effective communications, as proper two -way communication

means explanations, question, criticism both up and down and not only one way.

- They are invariably hard taskmasters and workaholics and may not be able to get best from the people working under them.

- They carry work home.

- They do not believe in team effort.

- These people are always rushing around and looking busy.

- They appraise their subordinates usually looking at their faults.

- They are mostly self centered and may not be prepared to take decisions with the organization's interest in mind.

When the Kundalini energy or the energy of the super cosmic force lying just below the spinal chord in the triangular bone known as sacrum bone, is awakened during the process of Self-Realization, rises through the central channel piercing the six chakras on her way. After she pierces the fontanel bone area, one feels cool breeze or vibration in his or her palm and top of the head. This brings forth a new dimension in the human personality of collective at the same time a very compassionate and peaceful person. This brings about a transformation in the individual and he begins to exhibit the beautiful qualities inherent in every chakra which gets reflected in his everyday activities in the office or managerial sphere as well. It may sound fantastic but it has happened to people from all walks of life around the walks life around the world- to scientists, physicians, engineers, professors, and common man. To experience Sahaja yoga one should open one's mind and heart to receive the blessings.

ENERGY CENTERS OR CHAKRAS AND THEIR EFFECT ON BEHAVIORAL PATTERN:-

1. The first chakra, which is mooladhara, gives us qualities of moral values like innocence, purity, wisdom and auspiciousness.

2. The second chakra, the swadishtan chakra gives us the power of creativity.

3. The third chakra known as nabhi grants us satisfaction, peace, generosity, welfares and determines our relationship with our spouse. It also controls our success in business and prosperity with honesty.

4. The fourth chakra known as anahata chakra gives us security, power of pure love and determines our relationship with our parents.

5. The fifth chakra known as vishudhi chakra determines our personality how we talk sweetly, aggressively or diplomatically and how pure is our relationship with opposite sex.

6. The sixth known as agnya chakra gives us the power to forgive others.

7. The seventh chakra known as sahasrar chakra is the integration of all chakras. Here all the qualities represented in the physical, mental, emotional and spiritual aspects of the human being gets integrated and he begins to pour forth the divinity in him in all his actions.

Chapter 18

Sahaja Yoga and Music

When the child is in the mother's womb, the all-pervading power or the Primordial Energy enters the child's brain. The human brain evolves into the shape of a prism with three sides and a base. When the energy enters, it passes through the surfaces of the brain at the fontanel bone area into the medulla oblongata which is the lower brain structure that's continuous with the spinal cord and controls functions such as respiration, circulation, etc, it splits into two forming the two subtle energy channels – the Ida nadi and the Pingla nadi. Our nervous systems at the gross level consist of the central nervous system and the autonomic nervous system, including the parasympathetic and sympathetic nervous systems on both sides of the body.

The residual energy from these processes settles into the triangular-shaped sacrum bone at the base of the spine as the reflection of the Primordial feminine energy. This is the Kundalini energy. These energy channels are subtle and invisible, just as the energy itself is subtle and invisible.

Before the residual energy settles down as the "Kundalini," the energy flow forms specific energy centers at specific points along the three energy channels.

Each of these energy centers is associated with specific functions and qualities. These can be strengthened through enlightenment which is brought about by awakening the kundalini energy within us and allowing it to work out within our nervous system.

This powerful Kundalini energy is dormant in us unless it's awakened through specific spiritual techniques or under the guidance of expert spiritual gurus. Once awakened, this energy, which is placed in the triangular sacrum bone, rises and passes through six energy centers that are distributed along the central nervous system. This energy establishes a connection with the cosmic energy or the all-pervading divine energy once it reaches the fontanel bone area. And once this connection is established, the energy centers vibrate in resonance with the Kundalini and cosmic energy, and one can actually experience the vibrations of the energy centers through the nerve endings on the fingers and toes. This energy awakening and sensation of the vibration of the chakras is the actualization of spiritual awakening in human beings.

This awakening provides several benefits, including the ability to understand your energy centers and remove imbalances and obstacles that are the root cause of all our physical, mental and emotional problems in life. After spiritual awakening, you become relaxed. You gain tremendous inner powers and energy that will empower you to solve all problems and lead a healthy, happy and peaceful life.

The seven basic swaras or musical notes of an octave have a one-to-one correspondence with these chakras.

The lower most chakra, the Muladhara Chakra is associated with the swara "sa"; that means, the practice of chanting this particular musical note will have impact on awakening or activation of this particular chakra. Similarly, the chakras successively upwards in this direction namely, the Swadhisthana, Manipura, Anahata,

Vishuddhi, Agnya and the top-most Sahasrara Chakra... have correspondence respectively with the swaras "re", "gad" "ma", "pa", "dhal" and "in".

Indian classical music has twelve notes. These twelve notes are used for absorption and energizing of the subtle system. These notes were the result of contemplation by the rashes and minis in the ancient times. Sa is from peacock, re is from bull, gad is from sheep, ma is from cuckoo, dha is from horse and in is from elephant. In Indian classical music they are known as normal notes. Besides this there are five other notes, flat re which is between normal sa and re, flat ga between normal re and ga, sharp ma between normal ma and pa, flat dha between pa and dha and flat ni between normal Dha and ni Sa and pa are static. Thus in all there are twelve notes in Indian classical music.

The normal notes Sa is for Mooladhar, Re is for Swadhishtan, ga is for Nabhi, Ma is for Anahat, Pa is for Vishudhi, Dha is for Agnya, and Ni stands for Sahasrar chakra. Sa is for left, right and central Mooladhar. Flat re is for left swadhishtan, and normal re is for central and right Swadhishtan, Flat ga is for left Nabhi while normal ga is for central and right Nabhi, Ma is for central and left heart, sharp ma represents right heart,

Pa is static and common for left Vishuddhi central and right vishuddhi, flat Dha is for right Agnya and normal Dha for central and left Agnya because at Agnya the left channel and right channels cross each other. Ni is for Sahasrar.

Each musical note carries a particular frequency. The frequency of Shadja or Sa is 240 and the related musical instrument is Shehanai; that of komal Rishabh Re is 254   2/17 while that of Shudha Rishabh Re is 270 and the related musical instrument is Veena; komal Gandhar or Ga is 288 that of Shudha Gandhar Ga is 301 17/43 and the related musical instrument is Santur; the frequency of Shudha Madhyam is 320 and Teevra Madhyam is 338 14/17 and the related musical instrument is the tabla; the frequency of Pancham or Pa is 360 and the instrument is Flute; the frequency of Komal Dhaivat or Dha is 381 3/17 and Shudha Dhaivat Dha is 405 and the musical instrument is Sarod and lastly Komal Nishad Ni the frequency is 432, Shudha Nishad Ni is 452 4/43 and the related musical instrument is Sitar.

Chakras and Bija Mantras

As a tree is contained in the seed, so also the power of a Mantra lies potentially in a Bija mantra. Just as the tree grows out of a seed, so also a mantra evolves from Bija mantra. Hence Bija mantras are the source of creation. Realizing the potencies of the Bija mantras, the saints and sages, rishis and munis devised mantras. When properly intoned the mantras have the power to activate the creative forces and produce the desired results. Divine protection and guidance are the general characteristics of all seed mantras. Each of them has its own specific transformative power. Bija mantras contain the potential of the Divine to manifest into a grand tree of spiritual illumination. They are like the engines pulling a train, and therefore they are often called as Shakti mantras. Om is the Bija mantras of universal consciousness.

Vaikhari or the power of speaking was made to have the transformative potential by the realized people, by framing mantras containing the bija mantras that are related to each chakra or energy centre. Every letter of the Sanskrit language is a mantra, that emanated from the meditative contemplations of the yogis and they have all come from the sound that emanates when the kundalini energy moves within a human being. When Kundalini energy moves it emanates a sound like sha..sh..sh..at the Mooladhara chakra. At every chakra it emits different sounds. To awaken the kundalini energy, the bija mantra is Reem. Shri Mataji once said in her talk in 1988 at Pune, India, that "Ra" is the energy Radha. One who sustains the energy is Radha. She is Mahalaxmi that is why She sustains the Kundalini. "Eee" is the Primordial Mother, and "Ra" is the energy that is kundalini. So "Reem" means that you have the energy passing through the body towards the Primordial Being.

All the petals of the seven chakras, have a particular letter which was seen and heard by the great Rishis during meditation. These letters are charged with the specific power of that particular petal and when chanted give the desired result.

The Mooladhara chakra or the Pelvic Plexus is placed below the sacrum bone and controls the excretory functions, as well as sexual activity, and exerts a general control on the left sympathetic nervous system. The Bija mantra of this chakra is "Lam". It has four petals which carry the sound of four bija aksharas namely, Wam, Sham, Sham, Sam. Influence of these sounds affect the prostate gland, vas deferens, Cervix of the uterus, and fallopian tubes. Sounds affecting this chakra or can be altered or positively induced to promote its inherent qualities of innocence, wisdom, chastity, sense of direction, balance, auspiciousness, simplicity, joy and purity. This is related to the Earth element and connected to the nose or sense of smell.

The Swadhishthana chakra or the Aortic Plexus is placed above the sacrum bone and plays an important role in controlling the abdominal organs such as the liver, kidneys and the large intestines. The Bija mantra of this chakra is "Wam". It has six petals which correspond to the six bija aksharas of Bam, Bham, Mam, Yam, Ram, Lam. This chakra has the power of sustenance or the Dharna Shakti. The reproductive organs of a woman are also partly controlled by this center. Being governed by the water element it is related to the tongue. Music related to this center can influence, kidneys, liver, pancreas, spleen and the lower abdomen. This center caters to the creative instincts of a person and this is the center that is focused for inducing qualities of creativity, pure attention, pure

The third Chakra is the Nabhi Chakra or the Colic plexus which controls the stomach, the pancreas and many other organs around the solar plexus. The Bija mantra is "Ram". It has ten petals which emit the sound of the bija aksharas which are Dam, Dham, Nam, Tam, Tham, Dam, Dham, Nam, Pam , Fam. This chakra has the power of transformation promote qualities like, complete satisfaction, generosity, peace and contentment, righteousness or Dharma, inner sense of morality, evolution, sense of dignity, and that of a good host. The chakra carries the fire element and is connected to the eyes.

The Anahata chakra which is the fourth chakra is the Cardiac Plexus and supplies air, blood and vibrations. The Bija mantra is "Yam" and has twelve petals carrying the sounds of the Bija aksharas such as Kam, Kham, Gam, Gham, Gam, Cham, Chham, Jam, Zam, Nyam, Tam, Tham. This chakra enhances the Divinity and Immunity power in children upto 12 years through the Thymus gland, which produces T-Lymphocytes and B-Lymphocytes. Music and ragas carrying the frequency of this chakra can promote compassion, pure love, complete sense of security, confidence, a joy of the spirit. It helps in nourishing the anti-bodies. Being connected to the air element this chakra is related to skin or a sense of touch.

The Vishuddhi chakra or the Cervical plexus which is the fifth chakra is governed by the Bija mantra "Ham". It has sixteen petals which respond to the sounds of the bija aksharas, Am, Aam, Im, Iim, Um, Uum, Rum, Ruum, Lrum, Lruum, Em, Aim, Aum, Oum, Am, Ah. Vishuddhi chakra which is a Divine confluence of the five elements and controller of five sense organs.

i.e. pancha tanmatras and pancha gnyanendriyas – nose with the earth element carrying smell or gandha tanmatra; the tongue works for the water element carrying the taste or rasa tanmatra; the eyes work for the fire element carrying vision or the teja tanmatra; ears work for the ether element carrying the shabda tanmatra; and skin works for the air element carrying the sparsha tanmatra. Vishuddi chakra is the Divine door of vocal music. This centre is also important for its control over the hands. Its qualities are divine diplomacy, detachment, witness state, collective consciousness, self-esteem, pure relationships, connection with the whole and Madhurya. It is connected to the space element or Akasha and hence connected to the ears.

The Agnya chakra or the Optic Chiasm is located at the base of the brain, and sits behind the forehead. The Bija mantra is "Om" and has two petals carrying the sounds of Ham and ksham. When the kundalini passes the Agnya chakra, our mental activity ceases, silence and enlightenment takes place. The Agnya chakra governs pineal and pituitary glands, Hypothalamus, Retina, Optic Chiasm and the optic lobes. The cleansing of this chakra promotes vision and light into life which brings the qualities of humility, forgiveness, dissolution of the ego, conditionings and false ideas. This chakra controls the sense of sankalpa – vikalpa. knowledge, inspiration, observation, power of concentration, Aesthetics and arts.

The Seventh chakra is the Sahasrar chakra in the limbic area which looks like a lotus of a thousand petals. Its Bija mantra is "Om" and it has no sound, but a pure

Anahat naad- the throbbing in a purest form and in the heart there is A La Ta La Ta A La. Its physical expression is the thousand nerves distributed under the surface of the skull. It is the integration of all the lower chakras and their power. It integrates all the chakras, and there is an absolute perception of reality as it is, on our central nervous system, and brings about a state of thoughtless awareness.

Bija mantras contain the potential of the Divine to manifest into the grand tree of spiritual illumination. When a person listens to music after his kundalini has been awakened and the chakras have been enlightened, he listens to music not through his ears but though the chakras. Chakras become the ears and kundalini ascends followed by spiritual emancipation. This is Sahaja yoga, the yoga for the whole world discovered by Her Holiness Shri Mataji Nirmala Devi

Chapter 19

Sahaja Yoga and Treatment of Diseases

Sahaj Yoga as rediscovered by Mataji Nirmala Devi aims at achieving holistic health care for people. The science focuses on awakening the dormant primordial energy (the Kundalini), whereby a flow of subtle cool cosmic vibrations in the body is achieved which nourishes and rejuvenates each and every cell of the body. As late Dr Umesh Rai, director of International Sahaj Yoga Research and Health Centre at Vashi Navi Mumbai had discovered, "As a result of meditation, which is the basic aim of Sahaj, the body manufactures certain fluids which have curative powers, which help in overcoming the most severe of ailments."

Dr Rai has researched at the Lady Hardinge Medical College and Associated Hospitals, New Delhi, on the role of Sahaj Yoga in the treatment of psychosomatic diseases.

He maintains that while with the advancement of the medical sciences, infectious diseases have been wiped out and heart and kidney transplants are quite successful, scientists have yet to find an answer for the treatment of psychosomatic diseases which are on the increase in the developed as well as the developing countries. Some such diseases are hypertension, migraine, bronchial asthma, epilepsy and others.

"The doctor of today practicing modern allopathic medicine has entered a stage of superspeciality whereby they appoint separate parts of the body to be treated by a specialist. Due to this approach doctors are not able to view disease as a disturbance to the whole organism. They treat a particular part of the body without taking into consideration the psychological and social aspects of the patients illness", says Rai. " One could be physically fit, but emotional problems or social isolation could make a person very sick."

He advises recourse to the ancient Indian scriptures like the Patanjali's Yoga Sutra that mentioned yoga as the most essential technique to keep the body and mind healthy. This is true even today but there is a need for integration that is not merely inner life but covers external life as well. "For yoga to be more relevant today, it needs to touch both the physical and mental aspects of health, which is encapsulated in the Sahaj Yoga. This science borders on all that which one is born with," says he.

It is based on our subtle nervous system. When the dormant primordial energy present as three and a half coils in the triangular sacrum bone gets activated on doing Sahaj Yoga, it ascends and activates one's six subtle chakras and piercing through Brahmarandhra, it unites with the all pervading cosmic energy." And with this actualization in the limbic area of the brain, subtle cool vibrations start flowing from both palms and the top of the head and in this vibratory awareness, one can feel what chakras are blocked, and can also work out their correction to cure different diseases.

To verify some of the claims of Sahaj Yoga, a systematic research study was organized in the physiology and medicine department of Lady Hardinge Medical College and Associated Hospitals in New Delhi. The research projects studied were psychological effects of Kundalini awakening by Sahaj Yoga and the effect of Sahaj practice on psychosomatic diseases like hypertension and bronchial asthma.

Says Ellerbee, the most important aspect of this science is to achieve a state of thoughtlessness. "Which is the most difficult of things to achieve? But once you get your mind free, you gradually begin to feel a calm stillness within," says she.

The International Sahaj Yoga centre at CBC Belapur founded and started by Shree Mataji Nirmala Devi is a unique centre of its kind in the world, where treatment is done by vibratory awareness, developed by Sahaj yoga meditation. . .Besides Indians, people from United States, UK, Switzerland, Belgium, Austria, New Zealand, Australia and several other countries of the world are admitted and treated for various health conditions. Today this centre has more international visitors than Indians.

Narrating about a rare recovery of a patient, S S Agarwal from Delhi Dr. Rai in his interview with the Indian express said, "His was a case of chronic renal failure, for which doctors had ruled out all treatment, except ongoing dialysis. By applying Sahaj yoga, we aroused his Kundalini energy (which is a dormant energy at the base of the spine) and directed it towards the kidney to clear his blocked chakras." Today, Agarwal's medical reports indicate near normalcy.

Etienne Loyson, a 62 year old architect from Belgium, is just spell-bound, "Earlier I had high blood pressure. Doctors abroad had suggested taking several tablets ongoing as the only treatment method. But today, with Sahaj yoga treatment and the blessing of Shree Mataji Nirmala Devi, I am full of energy. I have stopped all medicines and I feel I am just 30 years old."

Katherine Reid from England (who suffered from irritable bowels syndrome) is a happy woman today, in contrast to her life previously when she had to take several medicines prior to her arrival in Navi Mumbai. "I feel much better having stopped my medication completely. My health has improved by about eighty per cent." Anna Kargaity, a Canadian who suffered from depressive psychosis is full of smiles today. "I now have a positive outlook towards life, being able to develop my own personality and express my feelings", she says. Similar benefits were highlighted by Belinda from Australia, Kumar from Canada, Bryan from USA and others.

On being asked as to why so many foreigners are coming to India, when advanced medicines are available with doctors of modern medicine all over the world, Dr. Rai added, "The doctors abroad don't have a treatment for the psyche of human being, except giving tranquillizers, sedatives and anti-depressant drugs. These are not only harmful, but also habit-forming. In view of this, Sahaj yoga, which can control the psyche of human being by meditation, has become very popular to the treatment and prevention of psychosomatic diseases like bronchial asthma, migraine, irritable bowel syndrome, infertility, multiple sclerosis and sodalities, to name a few. It is all due to the blessings of Shree Mataji Nirmala Devi, who founded Sahaj Yoga centre, and has enlightened thousands of people all over the world."

Sahaja Yoga is a cognitive therapy as well as curative breakthrough:

- It enables the individuals to intervene on the central nervous system and the state of their centers and channels of energy (chakras).

- It gives access to a subtle form of energy, kundalini. This energy can be accessed through almost effortless, natural techniques to bring balance and health in one is mind, body, and emotions.

- It raises the human awareness to a new dimension of collective consciousness which enables the individual to feel the energetic state of another person and help in improving it.

Some of the research confirmed benefits of Sahaja Yoga:

1. Sahaja Yoga has achieved tremendous success in treatment of innumerable chronic fatal diseases. Recent medical investigations reveals that individuals suffering from hypertension, cancer, chronic asthma, epilepsy, diabetes, arthritis and heart ailments have recovered completely after practicing Sahaja Yoga meditation.

2. Another astounding medical breakthrough documented from Australia is the cure and

treatment of AIDS cases by using Sahaja Yoga techniques.

3.   The healing effects of Sahaja Yoga have encouraged doctors and others in the caring professions to develop centers where Sahaja Yoga techniques would be applied to patients suffering from a variety of ailments.

4.   In fact, Dr. Valentina Gostera, who works as a pediatrician in general hospital in the Soviet Union, was able to give her two patients a new lease of life. One was a child with an 11-inch liver, where all diagnostic and surgical recommendations made by a team of doctors did not yield results. Finally she treated the child on the principles of Sahaja Yoga and the liver started to heal gradually. After a few weeks, the liver shrunk back to its normal size. The same doctor at a party treated another case of fatal asthma, where the man who collapsed after an asthma attack, began to feel an easing of the symptoms. He had been suffering asthma for the past 45 years and now he has fully recovered.

5.   Also, Dr. Chugh's pioneering work presents experimental evidence to show the beneficial effects of Sahaja Yoga on essential hypertension and bronchial asthma. Hyper tension being due to excess of right-sided activity, Sahaja yoga practice corrects this imbalance in the neural communication. Similarly, asthma is said to be due to construction in the cardiac center on the right side. Thus relieving this construction causing asthma leads to instantaneous relief.

6. Further, diabetes, cancer of the blood, kidney troubles and heart attacks, according to Sahaja yoga being disorders as a result of excess mental activity, and skin disorder, anorexia, angina and epilepsy being caused due to a tendency to dwell on the past or indulge in depression, therapy would essentially be directed to rectify these imbalances and to attain peace within.

How does meditation bring about these effects?

Sahaja yoga meditation triggers a process within the autonomic nervous system, a complex set of nerves that governs the function of all the organs of our body. Imbalance within this system, is the cause of both physical and psychological illness. The process of meditation rebalances this system thereby allowing our natural healing processes to revitalize and rejuvenate diseased organs.

The ancient yoga tradition triggers the inner healing process in terms of seven subtle energy centers that exist within our body. Each of these centers governs a specific set of organs, and aspects of our psychology and spirituality. Imbalanced function of these centers results in abnormal function of any aspect of our being (physical, mental or spiritual) that relates to the imbalanced centre.

Meditation through the specific process that involves the awakening of the innate, nurturing energy, the "kundalini" causes it to rise from its position in the sacrum bone and pierce through each of the chakras, causing each of them to come into a state of balance and alignment. The chakras are rejuvenated and nourished by the kundalini's ascent. As the kundalini reaches the brain and the chakras within it, mental tensions are neutralized. An inner state of mental calm is established. This inner silence becomes a source of inner peace that neutralizes the stresses of daily life, enhancing creativity, productivity and self-satisfaction.

BRAIN WAVES

In order to try and understand what it is about the Sahaja Yoga meditation that makes it special some sophisticated brain imaging technology was used. A pilot study of advanced sahaja yoga meditators using a QEEG (quantitative electro encephelo gram) has yielded some very interesting results. This method is able to produce two-dimensional maps of the electrical changes in the brain as the meditator enters into the state of meditation. The study was conducted in Australia on a small group of meditators who were each asked to meditate while wearing a QEEG head cap designed to pick up the tiny electrical signals produced by the brain.

They were instructed to sit quietly for some time, then to commence meditation and signal when they had definitely entered into the meditative state called "thoughtless awareness". The findings were fascinating: all three of the meditators displayed widespread changes in brainwave activity that became more intense as they meditated. Widespread, intense "alpha wave" activity occurred initially. Alpha wave activity is associated with relaxation and is thought to be a beneficial state. The remarkable thing, however, is that as the meditators signaled that they had entered into the state of mental silence, or "thoughtless awareness", another form of brain wave activity emerged which involved "theta waves" focused specifically in the front and top of the brain in the midline. Precisely at the time that the theta activity became prominent, the meditators reported that they experienced a state of complete mental silence and "oneness" with the present moment, a state which characterizes the sahaja yoga meditative experience.

There are several remarkable features about this pilot study which warrant further investigation.

First, very few meditation techniques have shown this kind of consistent change in the theta range suggesting that the technique may have a unique effect on the brain. We were only able to find one other study, out of several dozen published in the scientific literature, that showed changes of this nature. This study involved a group of Japanese Zen monks. Practitioners of sahaja yoga often claim to feel the chakras (energy centers) within the head open up as the meditative experience intensifies. They assert that it is this experience which is the essence of true meditation and that very few other meditation techniques enable the subject to repeatedly access this experience.

Second, it is very significant that the changes observed in the brain images occurred at the moment that the meditators reported experiencing the meditative state. This suggests that the QEEG method may make it possible to directly study mystical states of consciousness! The fact that these changes occurred within minutes rather than hours or longer suggests a relatively effortless or spontaneous process (as suggested by the name of the technique - "sahaja" is Sanskrit for "effortless").

Third, the focus of theta activity at the front of the head and top of the head, both in the midline, suggest that structures deep within the brain, possibly the limbic system, are being activated. The limbic system is responsible for many aspects of our subjective experiences, such as emotion and mood, so it is no surprise that meditation, which is traditionally associated with blissful states, might involve this part of the brain.

Finally, in speculation, the two areas of theta activity coincidentally correspond to the two main chakras in the brain, according to yogic tradition. The forehead chakra called "agnya" or "third eye" is located in the centre of the forehead while the chakra at the top of the head, is called "sahasrara" or "crown chakra" and is traditionally associated with the limbic system.

"What a great thing it would be if we in our busy lives could restore into ourselves each day for at least a couple of hours and

prepare our minds to listen to the voice of the great silence.

The divine radio is always singing if we could only make ourselves ready to listen to it, but it is impossible to listen without silence."

Mahatma Gandhi

Meditation is an eastern tool that offers western

health practitioners a new way of looking at health. While, for most of us, focusing on the absolute present moment is virtually impossible, it is this razor's edge of "thoughtless awareness" that the easterner seeks to cultivate and sustain in meditation. The vast inner silence of the thoughtless state leaves the mind uncluttered. By existing in that "space-between-the thoughts" one is neither enslaved to one's past nor confined to a predetermined future. The inner silence of meditation thus creates a naturally stress-free inner environment.

Is it possible for humans to live in the present moment? Yes, it is, and most of us encounter living examples of it regularly! Observe closely the next small child you encounter. They have no worried lines on their faces, are almost always playing and enjoying themselves, and rarely complain about bills, jobs, chores, etc. If one happens to have an unpleasant experience it is quickly forgotten and life goes on. They are naturally balanced, living-in-the-present, stress-free beings. Who has seen a toddler hold a grudge, worry about the next meal or even think about what they did yesterday or will do tomorrow? They are so focused on the present moment that they are entirely spontaneous, unpretentious and usually very happy. They are in a constant state of effortless meditation.

Living in the moment is not, however, a regression to immaturity. It is an evolutionary step in which we return to our childlike innocence and simplicity but in full awareness of ourselves, our place in society and our moral role and responsibility. How does one tap into and sustain a connection with the present moment? How does one escape the brainstorm of mental stress that we all experience? It is possible through the "sahaja yoga effect" Sahaja yoga meditation appears to offer a method by which each of us can tame the brainstorm, realize a state of peace and tranquility and begin to heal our body, mind and spirit.

Chapter 20

Recognitions from the world

- Shri Mataji was invited by the United Nations for four consecutive years to speak on ways to achieve world peace between 1989 - 94

- Shri Mataji was an official guest speaker at the Women's Conference in Beijing and was official guest of the Chinese Government to speak to the people of China in 1995

- Shri Mataji was nominated twice for the Nobel Peace Prize St. Petersburg, Russia (1993) [Appointed as Honorary Member of the Presidium of the Petrovska Academy of Art and Science. In the history of the Academy only 12 people have ever been granted this honor, Einstein being one of them]

- Romania(1995)[Awarded Honorary Doctorate in Cognitive Science]

- St Petersburg, Russia (1998)[Inaugurated the International conference of Medicine and self-Knowledge]

- Moscow(1989)[Shri Mataji had a meeting with the head of the Ministry of Health in USSR, following which Sahaja Yoga was granted full Government Sponsorship including funding for promotion of Scientific Research]

- Brazil(1994)[The Mayor welcomed Shri Mataji at the airport and presented her with the key to the city, and sponsored all of her programs]

- Italy(1996)[Declared "Personality of the Year" by Italian Government]

- London(1997)

- [Separate personal tributes paid to Shri Mataji from Claes Nobel (Grandnephew of Alfred Nobel) and Ayatollah Rouhani (leader of the Shia Moslems in Europe) at the Royal Albert Hall]

- India2001[Manav Ratna Award in Pune]

Chapter 21

A Vision for the Future

It is a very privileged place for you to enter, into the Sahasrara of the Virata (The Cosmic Whole), to reside in the brain as cells of Sahasrara. These are specially created cells through the working of the Swadhisthana. Passing through all the chakras, when they arrive at Sahasrara they are equipped to handle the brain's activity without getting involved with other elements in the body. The first thing that happens to a Sahaja Yogi at the Sahasrara level is that he becomes 'Beyond', (Atita). He transcends so many things; he goes beyond time, (Kalatita). Time is his slave. If you have to go somewhere then suddenly you discover that everything is working at the same time when you are able to do it. Like you are, say, to catch a train and you arrive late at the station, you find the train is late for you. Things work out in such a way that you feel they are all active for your complete convenient to go beyond time that is kalatitia.

Then you go beyond dharma (Dharmatita). That means dharma becomes part and parcel of your being. Nobody has to tell you, "you do this" or "you do that" - you just do it. Whatever you have to do, you do it. When you go beyond all these dharmas, that are the human dharmas - human dharma is that one's attention gets attracted either with lust, greed to something, and then one cannot draw one's attention away. Then the attention becomes 'dharmatita'. That means the attention loses its dharma. The dharma of the attention is such that we have to use the dharmas taught by the prophets to control it. Because we are coming (in evolution) from the lowest level. So these (lower) dharmas exist in our being and start showing, and when they attack us, then we have to have some measures with which to control them. So we build up our dharmas, OUR OWN SELF-REGULATION, and control them, those dharmas which have come to us from lower conditioning. This is the greatness of human beings, that they have made their own dharmas, established on top of the lower dharmas.

But with the Sahasrara ascent the attention loses that quality, which means you do not need to put dharmas, restrictions upon yourself. You do not have to discipline yourself, but you get disciplined automatically. The attention does not get attached to, or attacked by, anything whatsoever, it is so pure. Like water does not stay on the Lotus leaf, so you become 'Kalatita', you become 'Dharmatita'. You become 'Gunanita'. Means, you go beyond the three 'moods' (Gunas) with which you are born, left, right and centre.

The left one in the one by which you have emotional attachments of your attention. The second one (right) is the physical and the mental attachments. And the third one (centre), is the attachment to the dharma, attachment to be righteous and to make other righteous, of disciplining others and disciplining yourself... Where a person tries to control all his enemies of lust, anger, pride, vanity, attachments and greed.

All these restrictions on the attention get lost and you become a free person of complete wisdom. Your attention itself becomes dharmic. So you lose all your gunas and you become 'Satgunis', means virtuous, not by discipline, but spontaneously. You become righteous Spontaneously.

So you reach a state which can be described with the word 'a' that means 'without'. So such a person is without thought, he does not think. Such person is without greed; such a person is without lust, devoid of it. Such a person is said to be 'ascesa': 'Out of which nothing is left out'. Like when you want to make a vacuum, you go on creating the vacuum. Reach any point and the vacuum cannot be completed because it reaches a point all the time where you find some part of it remains. You cannot have a complete vacuum. But such a person has a complete vacuum - a vacuum of all the negative, aggressive qualities - complete, they do not exist.

Such a person is an eternal being nobody can kill, nobody can harm, nobody can hurt. The hanger of anyone or respect of anyone does not touch such a person. He is not disturbed by insults or non-insults. He is not elated by prayers, because he is devoid of the capacity to enjoy the boons of the ego.

So at the third state he reaches he gets the blessing of the word 'Nih'. Nih is the first word of my name, but in Sanskrit, when you combine it with 'Mala', then it becomes 'Nirmala' (Pure). But the word is Nih...

...But this word nira or nih, is used in two forms... One for say: 'Without' or 'Devoid of'. Then another form is: 'The only', 'The absolute joy, nothing but joy. It is complete freedom. So you have all kinds of joys, as I told you before. You have Svananda - the joy of the spirit, then you have got Brahmanada - the joy of well-being. You have got Leelananda and Krishnananda - where you have the joy of the play. But when you reach the state of Sahasrara it is NIRANANDA - means, sheer absolute joy. Although the name 'Nira' is my name, it means 'Absolute'. So when you put such an adjective before anything else it becomes absolute. Thus YOU become absolute. And when you are at that state of absolute then there is no place for anything Let us see what 'Absolute' is? That means it is not relative, it has no relative qualities. Absolute cannot be compared (Atuliya) it cannot be compared. It cannot relate to anything, it is absolute. It cannot be comprehended because it cannot be related to anything else through which we can comprehend. It is absolute. Whatever way you try to know it, you go away from the absolute. Wherever you try to analyze the absolute, you are away from it. So this is what at Sahasrara you get - 'Nirananda' (Sheer joy).

In different stages of Sahaja Yoga we had to start from 'Sarirananda', means the ananda (Joy) of the body; 'Manasananda', the joy of the 'Manas', the psyche. Then you can say 'Ahamkarananda', where you have to have the satisfaction of the ego. But the state that now has to be established within us is of 'Nirananda'. Then what is the question of fear? What is the question of talking about it? You cannot talk about it, because how will you relate it? I cannot say "It is like this, it is like that". There are no words to describe the Absolute.

Only by negation: 'not this, not this' and what remains is absolute. So you reach the state of absolute and that is the state a complete communication is established and in that communication you have nobody else but the absolute within you. That is the level to which you should aspire. That should be the ascent. We should be established within ourselves. We do not have to go to the Himalayas, we do not have to do anything drastic. Remaining in this world, we have to become the Absolute, the 'Only' (Kevalam). There is nothing like "How?" for it. You just become. You just become, like a flower becomes the fruit. It is all built in. Allow it to work out.

Just by surrendering you become. Surrender it and you will be surprised; you will be at the state where you will enjoy your absoluteness. It is absolute love, it is absolute compassion, it is absolute power. The words stops, the description stops. You just become the absolute and feel your absoluteness through it with the oneness. If somebody is not with you, you do not worry. There is no company needed. You are alone enjoying the Absolute. Only there can you also enjoy the Absolute in others, in the best form, without seeing anything else but the Absolute.

May God Bless You."

Sahasrar Puja -1985.

Bibliography

1.References from speeches by Shri Mataji Nirmala Devi as detailed below:

- Divine Discrimination –Chapter 5 – Talk on 28th May 1990 at San Diego

- Likes and Dislikes – Chapter 6 – Talk at Rahuri on 25th December 1987

- Sanctity of Marriage –Chapter 6 – Talk at Cabella on 16th September 2000

- Giving and Generosity – Chapter 7- Talk at Ganapatiphule on 25th December 2001.

- Trust – Chapter 9- Talk at Cabella on Guru Puja on 23rd July 2000

- Our growth is our concern- Chapter 10- Talk at cabella on Sahasrar Puja on 5th May 1996.

- Chapter 11- Speech on the occasion of Raksha Bandhan at London on 20th August 1988.

- Freedom – Talk at Cabella on 23rd August 1997.

- Intuition- Chapter 14- Talk at Pandharpur 29th February 1984

- Purity of Dedication to your Goal- Chapter 15- Mahasahasrar Puja Talk on 5th May 1984.

- Stress and Tension management through Sahaja Yoga- Chapter 17-Talk at Mumbai on 11th March 2000

- A vision for the future – Chapter 21 -Talk at Vienna on the occasion of Sahasrar Puja on 5th May 1985.

2. Chapter 18:

1. Neki, J.S., "Sahaja: an Indian ideal of mental health", *Psychiatry*,

Vol. 38, No. 1, Feb 1975, pp. 1-10.

2. Maslow, A., *Religions, Values, and Peak Experiences*, The Viking Press, New York, 1972.

3. Holmes, D.S., "The influence of meditation, versus rest, on

physiological arousal", in West, M.A., (ed.), *The Psychology of*

Meditation, Clarendon Press, Oxford, 1987.

4. Rai, U.C. et al., "Some effects of Sahaja Yoga and its role in the prevention of stress disorders", *Journal International Medical Sciences Academy*, 1988.

5. Panjwani, U., Selvamurthy, W., Singh, S.H., Gupta, H.L.,Mukhopadhyay, S., Thakur, L., "Effect of Sahaja yoga meditation on auditory evoked potentials (AEP) and visual contrast sensitivity (VCS) in epileptics", *Applied Psychophysiology & Biofeedback*, Vol. 25, No. 1, March 2000, pp. 1-12.

6. Rai, op. cit. (Ref 9).

7 Manocha, R., "Why Meditation?", *Australian Family Physician*, Vol. 29, No. 12, Dec 2000. pp. 1135-1138r 18:

3. Life sketch from www.sahajayoga.org and book titled My Memoires by Babamama

4. Pictures with messages on them – Oneness messages by Rasha, author of the Book "The Divine Wisdom of Oneness"

Our Humble Pranams at Your Holy Feet Param Pujya Shree Mataji

About the Author

Sahaja yoga, a unique integration of the ancient knowledge of Kundalini or the primordial energy and its actualization through the practice of meditation techniques, is what Saraswati Raman, a Banker by profession, has found to be the secret to self-unfoldment and transformation as she passionately explores in this book. She looks at how through introspection in moments of thoughtless awareness at normal everyday emotions of guilt, forgiveness, giving and generosity, likes and dislikes, trust, criticism, and creating positive patterns of thought and behavior can allow a person to make that all important shift in consciousness. She owes this all important nirmal vidya to her spiritual teacher Shri Mataji Nirmala Devi, who has been transforming millions of people all over the world by establishing the lost connection with the all pervading cosmic power that gives an individual a new energy, meaning and purpose in all that they do.

Saraswati Raman who has been practicing meditation since her college days, took up Sahaja yoga ten years ago, and life has changed dramatically for her. Her career got uplift, she could complete her ambition for an MBA degree with specialization in Banking and Finance. She even has an MD in Alternative medicine from the Indian Board for Alternative Medicine, Kolkata. As she emphasizes, when the kundalini awakening happens, there is an all-round integration of the personality, not only spiritual, but physical, mental, emotional, and at the intellectual levels as well.

Printed in Great Britain
by Amazon.co.uk, Ltd.,
Marston Gate.